The Celebrity Tweet Directory

Jeanne Harris

WILEY
Wiley Publishing, Inc.

The Celebrity Tweet Directory

Published by
Wiley Publishing, Inc.
10475 Crosspoint Blvd.
Indianapolis, IN 46256
www.wiley.com

For general information on our other products and services or to obtain technical support, please contact our Customer Care Department within the U.S. at (877) 762-2974, outside the U.S. at (317) 572-3993 or fax (317) 572-4002.

Wiley also publishes its books in a variety of electronic formats. Some content that appears in print may not be available in electronic books.

Library of Congress Control Number: 2009942823

WILEY

Credits

Senior Acquisitions Editor
Stephanie McComb

Technical Editor
Todd Siesky

Editorial Director
Robyn Siesky

Editorial Manager
Cricket Krengel

Vice President and Group Executive Publisher
Richard Swadley

Vice President and Executive Publisher
Barry Pruett

Business Manager
Amy Knies

Senior Marketing Manager
Sandy Smith

Project Coordinator
Katie Crocker

Graphics and Production Specialists
Elizabeth Brooks, Joyce Haughey,
Andrea Hornberger

Quality Control Technicians
Laura Albert, Lindsay Littrell

Indexing
Valerie Haynes Perry

About the Author

Jeanne Harris is a freelance consultant and contractor through her company Jeanne Harris Consulting. She currently is the principle design consultant and dealer at Chairadise. Jeanne worked as Business Development Director at Jupiterimages, was the Marketing and Sales director, Partner development Manager and Consultant at Photoworkshop.com and DoubleExposure.com.

Special Thanks

It takes a village to create a successful book and this is certainly no exception. Multiple teams at Wiley came together to make this happen at breakneck speed. It's truly amazing.

Mike Trent, you are an artistic rock star on covers and category opener art for this book and across the board. You make the ideas come to life. Many, many thanks.

Beth Brooks, you created this design and it's bright, cheerful, colorful (even for a two color book), and most of all user friendly. You zero in on the details and leave no stone unturned and it shows in your work. Thank you, thank you, thank you.

Todd Siesky, you are a fact checking machine. Through rain, snow, sleet, shine and lack of sleep you reviewed and verified these entries.

Stephanie McComb, you are the acquisitions editor of the gods. Your guidance, advice, and assistance were immeasurable.

Robyn Siesky, your editing and project management brought this book up to the level. "40 characters or less including spaces" is the new mantra.

Contents

Contents

Introduction

What are you doing?

With that humble, even mundane, question, a company, a network, and a phenomenon were born.

What are you doing?

It's a question that seems crafted to elicit nothing but the most trivial of replies: I just woke up; I'm having bacon and eggs for breakfast; I'm in a boring meeting; I'm taking my kids to school; I'm going to bed.

But a funny thing has happened in the three years or so that Twitter has been part of the social networking scene: Twitter users took the original What are you doing? question and morphed it into something more along the lines of What's happening now? That seemingly subtle change has made all the difference because it opens up a world of new questions: What are you reading? What great idea did you just come up with? What interesting person did you just see or have dinner with? What great information did you stumble upon on the Web? What hilarious video would you like to share?

At one time, Twitter's most notable users were a tech blogger and a mid-20s female known for strapping a Web Cam to her head and fawning over Apple gadgets. Today, the top users are literally the famous: Ashton Kutcher, Ellen DeGeneres, Britney Spears and Lance Armstrong to name just a few. Celebrities tend to open up on Twitter in a way never seen in tabloid magazines.

Twitter offers real-time tabloid drama, on-set spoilers and provides a direct connection with the real person behind the celebrity brand. This directory will help you quickly and easily find out which of your celebrity favorites uses Twitter.

Who should read this book? You!

Some books are aimed squarely at specific types of people: beginners, programmers, left-handers, or whatever. Not this book.

The Celebrity Tweet Directory is for anyone and everyone! This book targets the millions of you already on Twitter or those of you new to Twitter who want to see what's happening with friends, family and your favorite celebrities. Whether you're a teen, a grandparent, or anyone in between, this portable directory helps you quickly discover what's truly happening in Hollywood, on Wall Street, or in Washington by following your favorite celeb, politician, and athlete. This book is divided by category with the celebrities listed in alphabetical order to easily find your favorites. This directory also aims to weed out the fake celebrity twitter accounts, providing only the real and verified Twitter handles, saving you the hassle and time of weeding through celebrity poser accounts.

Happy Twittering!

The changing Twitter user

While we have researched and verified everything possible in this directory, the people using and stats of Twitter change multiple times daily—adding or deleting accounts, adjusting their handles, follower number changing, etc... There is a chance that the Twitter celebrity you're looking for may not be on Twitter anymore or may have changed their handle to avoid copycats. We've done everything to avoid this, but you can just never tell with a celebrity.

Actors/Directors/Producers

Movie Actors/Actresses

Jessica Alba
@JessMAlba
Followers: 11,933
Fantastic Four

Tom Cruise
@TomCruise
Followers: 181,923
Tropic Thunder, Mission Impossible 1-3

Stephen Baldwin
@FREAKSB
Followers: 3,205
The Usual Suspects, Biosphere

Hugh Dancy
@hughdancyy
Followers: 406
Confessions of a Shopaholic

Elizabeth Banks
@ElizabethBanks
Followers: 65,741
The 40 Year Old Virgin

Kat Dennings
@OfficialKat
Followers: 39,237
Nick and Norah's Infinite Playlist

Kristen Bell
@IMKristenBell
Followers: 74,646
Forgetting Sarah Marshall

Danny DeVito
@Danny_DeVito
Followers: 256,637
Romancing the Stone, Matilda

Celebrity Tweets
Anyone see Angels & Demons? Tom Hanks ruined it for me when he told Stephen Colbert anti-matter is harmless. A shaken soda is more scary.
@Mark_Wahlberg (Mark Wahlberg)

Russell Brand
@rustyrockets
Followers: 655,826
Forgetting Sarah Marshall

Peter Facinelli
@peterfacinelli
Followers: 1,315,126
Twilight, New Moon

Jim Carrey
@JimCarrey
Followers: 64,688
Ace Ventura series, The Truman Show

Mia Farrow
@mia_farrow
Followers: 1,707
Rosemary's Baby, Be Kind Rewind

Actors/Directors/Producers

Celebrity Tweets
"Starry, starry night. Paint your palette blue and grey, Look out on a summer's day, With eyes that know the darkness in my soul."
@RachelleLefevre (Rachelle Lefevre)

Tom Felton
@TomFelton
Followers: 208,577
Harry Potter series

Tom Hanks
@tomhanks
Followers: 70,238
Philadelphia, Castaway

Carrie Fisher
@CarrieFFisher
Followers: 21,833
Star Wars trilogy, When Harry Met Sally

Anne Hathaway
@hathaway_anne
Followers: 14,863
Ella Enchanted, The Devil Wears Prada

Jane Seymour Fonda
@Janefonda
Followers: 55,143
Nine to Five, Monster-in-Law

Mariel Hemingway
@Marielhemingway
Followers: 187,019
Manhattan

Celebrity Tweets
And I just want to add f**k you paparazzi for invading our privacy. The laws are changing here in CA and that is a 50 grand fine!
@mrskutcher (Demi Moore)

Danny Glover
@mrdannyglover
Followers: 1,236,879
Lethal Weapon 1-4

Tyler Hilton
@tylerhilton
Followers: 26,830
Walk the Line

Whoopi Goldberg
@WhoopiGoldberg1
Followers: 2,298
Ghost

Timothy Hutton
@timhutton
Followers: 3,015
Taps, Ordinary People, Last Holiday

Celebrity Tweets
Best of luck to @EdNorton who is running the NY Marathon today!
@KevinSpacey (Kevin Spacey)

Eddie Izzard
@eddieizzard
Followers: 1,295,337
Ocean's Twelve and Thirteen

Lindsay Lohan
@lindsaylohan
Followers: 161,213
The Parent Trap, Mean Girls

Celebrity Tweets
If I were king I would ban those boxes on forms that ask you what race you are. There would be only one box and the answer would be"human".
@TimmyDaly (Tim Daly)

Hugh Jackman
@RealHughJackman
Followers: 499,040
X-Men series, Wolverine

Virginia Madsen
@madlyv
Followers: 6,708
Sideways, The Number 23

Val Kilmer
@ValEKilmer
Followers: 3,833
Top Gun

Gilles Marini
@GillesMarini
Followers: 12,000
Sex and the City: The Movie

Celebrity Tweets
As you get older the pickings get slimmer but the people sure don't.
@CarrieFFisher (Carrie Fisher)

Larry The Cable Guy
@GitRDoneLarry
Followers: 20,091
Delta Farce, Witless Protection

Steve Martin
@iamstevemartin
Followers: 1,861
The Shop Girl, Cheaper by the Dozen 1-2

Rachelle Lefevre
@RachelleLefevre
Followers: 160,566
Twilight, New Moon

Marlee Matlin
@MarleeMatlin
Followers: 29,103
Children of a Lesser God

Celebrity Tweets
Why is it that women's health is always the sacrificial lamb? Even under the Obama presidency!
@janefonda (Jane Seymour Fonda)

Actors/Directors/Producers

Celebrity Tweets
when I think of how many people aren't being punched in the face right now I'm proud of us. so many getting along so well. :)}}
@JimCarrey (Jim Carrey)

Rachel McAdams
@RachelMcAdams
Followers: 21,930
The Notebook, Wedding Crashers

Alex Pettyfer
@apet09
Followers: 748
Stormbreaker

Jason Mewes
@JayMewes
Followers: 49,654
Clerks, Jay and Silent Bob Strike Back

Denise Richards
@DENISE_RICHARDS
Followers: 1,368,828
Wild Things, Undercover Brother

Matthew Modine
@MatthewModine
Followers: 2,900
Full Metal Jacket, Married to the Mob

Emmy Rossum
@emmyrossum
Followers: 53,637
The Day After Tomorrow

Demi Moore
@mrskutcher
Followers: 2,310,625
Ghost, Charlie's Angels: Full Throttle

Michael Sheen
@michaelsheen
Followers: 60,185
Frost/Nixon, New Moon

Edward Norton
@EdwardNorton
Followers: 220,318
American History X, The Incredible Hulk

Kevin Spacey
@KevinSpacey
Followers: 1,423,844
The Usual Suspects, American Beauty

Celebrity Tweets
Why don't they have floatation devices fixed to airplanes 'black box'
@mia_farrow (Mia Farrow)

Simon Pegg
@simonpegg
Followers: 112,910
Shaun of the Dead

Mary Steenburgen
@MSteenburgen
Followers: 796
What's Eating Gilbert Grape, Elf

Ben Stiller
@RedHourBen
Followers: 712,046
Reality Bites, Zoolander

Verne Troyer
@VerneTroyer
Followers: 6,599
Austin Powers series

Channing Tatum
@channingtatum
Followers: 93,552
Coach Carter, G.I. Joe

Nia Vardalos
@NiaVardalos
Followers: 25,655
My Big Fat Greek Wedding

Elizabeth Taylor
@DameElizabeth
Followers: 185,475
Who's Afraid of Virginia Wolfe

Mark Wahlberg
@Mark_Wahlberg
Followers: 101,498
Boogie Nights

Celebrity Tweets
Wow..I just heard from Perez Hilton that Miley Cyrus thinks twitter should be banned from this universe..what do you think about that?
@JessMAlba (Jessica Alba)

Ashley Tisdale
@ashleytisdale
Followers: 2,294,202
Highschool Musical series

Marlon Wayans
@MARLONLWAYANS
Followers: 66,298
Scary Movie 1-2

TV Actors/Actresses

Kirstie Alley
@kirstiealley
Followers: 446,205
V, Cheers, Fat Actress

Aziz Ansari
@azizansari
Followers: 68,154
Parks and Recreation, Reno 911!

Pamela Anderson
@PamelaDAnderson
Followers: 90,423
Baywatch

Christina Applegate
@1capplegate
Followers: 297,198
Married... with Children, Samantha Who

Celebrity Tweets
I tweet a lot. Consider yourself forewarned.
@Alyssa_Milano (Alyssa Milano)

Adrienne Bailon
@Adrienne_Bailon
Followers: 214,330
The Cheetah Girls

David Blue
@DavidBlue
Followers: 74,409
Ugly Betty

Mischa Barton
@THEREALMISCHA
Followers: 118,536
The O.C.

Michele Boyd
@micheleboyd
Followers: 4,579
The Guild

Justine Bateman
@JustineBateman
Followers: 16,525
Family Ties

Rob Brydon
@RobBrydon
Followers: 86,844
Marion and Geoff, The Keith Barret Show

Amber Benson
@amber_benson
Followers: 31,505
Buffy the Vampire Slayer

Candace Cameron Bure
@candacecbure
Followers: 29,537
Full House

Celebrity Tweets
When sketches aren't on-line it almost always has to do with musical clearance issues.
@sethmeyers21 (Seth Meyers)

Valerie Bertinelli
@Wolfiesmom
Followers: 4,278
One Day at a Time

LeVar Burton
@levarburton
Followers: 1,455,447
Star Trek: The Next Generation

Michael Ian Black
@michaelianblack
Followers: 1,457,615
Ed

Adam Busch
@AdamBusch
Followers: 6,191
Buffy the Vampire Slayer

Amanda Bynes
@amandabynes
Followers: 163,431
All That, What I Like About You

John Cabrera
@johncabrera
Followers: 2,968
Gilmore Girls

Nick Cannon
@NickCannon
Followers: 1,383,000
All That

Michael Chiklis
@MichaelChiklis
Followers: 4,301
The Commish, The Shield

Tim Daly
@TimmyDaly
Followers: 2,395
Wings, Private Practice

Tony Danza
@TonyDanza
Followers: 46,720
Taxi, Who's the Boss?

Stacey Dash
@REALStaceyDash
Followers: 9,210
Celebrity Circus

Alan Davies
@alandavies1
Followers: 112,559
Jonathan Creek

Celebrity Tweets
Just got asked "team Jacob or team Edward?" by a bunch if girls. I answered "get off my lawn!" holding my shotgun. Too much?
@dannymasterson (Danny Masterson)

Margaret Cho
@margaretcho
Followers: 609,233
Drop Dead Diva

Chris Colfer
@chriscolfer
Followers: 53,123
Glee

Stephen Collins
@Bassisland
Followers: 1,666
7th Heaven

Felicia Day
@feliciaday
Followers: 1,574,211
Buffy the Vampire Slayer

India de Beaufort
@Indiadebeaufort
Followers: 1,502
The Basil Brush Show, One Tree Hill

Jeffrey Donovan
@Jeffrey_Donovan
Followers: 25,480
Burn Notice

Fran Drescher
@frandrescher
Followers: 39,948
The Nanny

Nathan Fillion
@NathanFillion
Followers: 304,031
Castle

Haylie Duff
@HaylieK
Followers: 59,745
Joan of Arcadia, 7th Heaven

Dave Foley
@DaveSFoley
Followers: 7,109
The Kids in the Hall, NewsRadio

Hilary Duff
@MissHilaryDuff
Followers: 89,073
Lizzie McGuire, Gossip Girl

Judah Friedlander
@JudahWorldChamp
Followers: 15,190
30 Rock

Eliza Dushku
@elizadushku
Followers: 286,596
Buffy the Vampire Slayer, Dollhouse

Soleil Moon Frye
@moonfrye
Followers: 1,300,624
Punky Brewster, Sabrina the Teenage Witch

Anthony Edwards
@anthonyedwards
Followers: 103,844
ER

Janina Gavankar
@janinaz
Followers: 14,529
The L Word

Jenna Elfman
@jennaonpurpose
Followers: 3,490
Dharma & Greg

Melissa Gilbert
@MelissaEGilbert
Followers: 24,650
Little House on the Prairie

Omar Epps
@omarepps
Followers: 581,930
House

Sara Gilbert
@THEsaragilbert
Followers: 37,222
Roseanne, The Big Bang Theory

Celebrity Tweets
I don't understand the expression same difference.
@langfordperry (Matthew Perry)

The Celebrity Tweet Directory

Summer Glau
@summer_glau
Followers: 11,634
Terminator: The Sarah Connor Chronicles

Selena Gomez
@selenagomez
Followers: 1,191,647
Wizards of Waverly Place

Brea Grant
@breagrant
Followers: 27,085
Heroes

Greg Grunberg
@greggrunberg
Followers: 1,276,681
Felicity, Heroes

Bear Grylls
@BearGrylls
Followers: 19,700
Man vs. Wild

Alyson Hannigan-Denisof
@alydenisof
Followers: 62,502
How I Met Your Mother

Danneel Harris
@DanneelHarris
Followers: 11,495
One Life to Live, One Tree Hill

David Harris
@BartonSmart
Followers: 908,410
Disaster Date

Neil Patrick Harris
@ActuallyNPH
Followers: 155,583
Doogie Howser, How I Met Your Mother

Kevin Hart
@KevinHart4real
Followers: 145,644
Comedy Central Presents

Celebrity Tweets
Just for the record, C.C. is AMAZING on set(and off). Everyone loves her! And you know that I wouldn't say it if it weren't true...
@Busyphilipps25 (Busy Philipps)

Harry Hamlin
@HarryRHamlin
Followers: 3,691
LA Law

Melissa Joan Hart
@MellyJHart
Followers: 30,004
Sabrina the Teenage Witch

Celebrity Tweets
Shaq just picked me up like a sack of potatoes...
@jeremypiven (Jeremy Piven)

Actors/Directors/Producers

David Hasselhoff
@DavidHasselhoff
Followers: 34,517
Knight Rider, Baywatch

David Henrie
@David_Henrie
Followers: 391,254
That's So Raven

David Hewlett
@dhewlett
Followers: 19,985
Stargate SG1, Stargate Atlantis

Kate Hewlett
@katehewlett
Followers: 7,369
Stargate Atlantis

Amanda Holden
@Amanda_Holden
Followers: 62,129
Britain's Got Talent

Alaina Huffman
@alainahuffman
Followers: 2,593
Painkiller Jane

Wesley Jonathan
@WesleyJonathan
Followers: 10,290
What I Like About You

Jamie Kennedy
@jamiekennedy
Followers: 45,401
The Ghost Whisperer

Mila Kunis
@MissMilaKunis
Followers: 17,952
That 70's Show, Family Guy

Ashton Kutcher
@aplusk
Followers: 4,012,189
That 70s Show, Punk'd

John Larroquette
@JohnLarroquette
Followers: 18,683
Night Court

Miracle Laurie
@miraclelaurie
Followers: 10,461
Dollhouse

David H.Lawrence XVII
@dhlawrencexvii
Followers: 7,872
Heroes

James Kyson Lee
@jameskysonlee
Followers: 18,718
Heroes

Celebrity Tweets

I've only broken 1 bone: my seventh vertebrae. In a diving accident. On my 18th birthday.
@donttrythis (Adam Savage)

Jared Leto
@jaredleto
Followers: 67,584
My So-Called Life

Lucy Liu
@itsLucyLiu
Followers: 21,152
Ally McBeal, Dirty Sexy Money

Blake Lively
@blakeclively
Followers: 147,214
Gossip Girl

Robert Llewellyn
@bobbyllew
Followers: 35,339
Red Dwarf

Lauren London
@MsLaurenLondon
Followers: 351,301
90210, Entourage

George Lopez
@georgelopez
Followers: 75,136
George Lopez, Reno 911!

Mario Lopez
@MarioLopezExtra
Followers: 75,886
Saved by the Bell, Extra

Demi Lovato
@ddlovato
Followers: 1,168,624
Camp Rock

Stephen Lunsford
@Lunsfuhd
Followers: 540
Kamen Rider, Dragon Knight

Allison Mack
@allisonmack
Followers: 15,936
Smallville

Danny Masterson
@dannymasterson
Followers: 1,249,974
That 70s Show

Jenny McCarthy
@JennyfromMTV
Followers: 61,086
The Bad Girl's Guide, In the Motherhood

Jennette McCurdy
@jennettemccurdy
Followers: 147,770
iCarly

Dean McDermott
@Deanracer
Followers: 24,156
Tori and Dean: Inn Love

Rose McGowan
@rosemcgowan
Followers: 43,115
Charmed

Joel McHale
@joelmchale
Followers: 1,526,435
The Soup, Community

Leighton Meester
@itsmeleighton
Followers: 261,738
Gossip Girl

Frankie Muniz
@frankiemuniz
Followers: 13,027
Malcolm in the Middle

Carlos Mencia
@carlosmencia
Followers: 10,647
Mind of Mencia

Olivia Munn
@oliviamunn
Followers: 102,167
Attack of the Show!

Seth Meyers
@sethmeyers21
Followers: 46,904
Saturday Night Live

Mary-Kate Olsen
@imMKOlsen
Followers: 85,609
Full House

Alyssa Milano
@Alyssa_Milano
Followers: 398,428
Who's the Boss, Charmed

Donny Osmond
@donnyosmond
Followers: 30,852
Dancing with the Stars

A.D. Miles
@80miles
Followers: 8,434
Dog Bites Man

Marie Osmond
@marieosmond
Followers: 16,217
Dancing with the Stars

Celebrity Tweets

my father said to me "a man has few great moments in his life-you have given me many" today is for you dad-and it even has your name on it!
@JohnStamos (John Stamos)

Shanna Moakler
@ShannaMoakler
Followers: 71,392
Pacific Blue

Joe Pantoliano
@NKMToo
Followers: 653
The Sopranos

Tahj Mowry
@Tahj_Mowry
Followers: 32,449
Smart Guy

Hunter Parrish
@HunterParrish
Followers: 17,519
Weeds

The Celebrity Tweet Directory

Holly Robinson Peete
@hollyrpeete
Followers: 20,155
21 Jump Street, Mr. Cooper

Kevin Pollak
@kevinpollak
Followers: 168,450
The Drew Carey Show, Shark

Matthew Perry
@langfordperry
Followers: 115,812
Friends

Jaime Pressly
@jpressly730
Followers: 13,251
My Name Is Earl

Celebrity Tweets
People who don't believe in evolution really shouldn't be allowed to get flu shots.
@rainnwilson (Rainn Wilson)

Busy Philipps
@Busyphilipps25
Followers: 6,863
Dawson's Creek, Cougar Town

Zachary Quinto
@ZacharyQuinto
Followers: 77,213
Heroes

Lou Diamond Phillips
@LouDPhillips
Followers: 7,323
SGU Stargate Universe, Numb3rs

Gloria Reuben
@Glo_Reuben
Followers: 279
ER

Celebrity Tweets
We r 43days away from the year 2010, Angelina Jolie & Jennifer Aniston r STILL fighting on the cover of tabloids. They moved on y can't we?
@NICKZANO (Nick Zano)

Jeremy Piven
@jeremypiven
Followers: 930,751
Entourage

Lisa Rinna
@lisarinna
Followers: 37,951
Days of our Lives, Melrose Place

Celebrity Tweets
As someone who was diagnosed with BC at 36 yrs old, I am especially angered by this. yet I still feel we need better ways of screening!
@1capplegate (Christina Applegate)

Actors/Directors/Producers

Michelle Rodriguez
@MRodOfficial
Followers: 11,891
Lost

Vanessa Simmons
@V_Simmons
Followers: 153,539
Run's House, The Guiding Light

Mark Salling
@Mark_Salling
Followers: 38,948
Glee

Jessica Simpson
@JessicaSimpson
Followers: 1,834,886
That 70's Show, Newlyweds

Adam Savage
@donttrythis
Followers: 109,697
MythBusters

Ashlee Simpson Wentz
@ashsimpsonwentz
Followers: 1,882,675
7th Heaven, Melrose Place

Kyra Sedgwick
@kyrasedgwick
Followers: 6,941
The Closer

Molly Sims
@MissMollySims
Followers: 592
Las Vegas

William Shatner
@WilliamShatner
Followers: 125,554
Star Trek, Boston Legal

Jaclyn Smith
@realjaclynsmith
Followers: 2,851
Charlie's Angels

Celebrity Tweets
Mom made me turn the depressing music off and put on "One Time" by my boy Justin Bieber. Why does he always put me in a good mood?
@selenagomez (Selena Gomez)

Grant Show
@GrantNoShow
Followers: 160
Melrose Place

Jamie-Lynn Spears
@JamieL_Spears
Followers: 7,981
All That, Zoey 101

Celebrity Tweets
..a thin but staunch prophylactic, the only barrier between me and cerebral anarchy. Hey, I think there's a song in there.......
@JohnLarroquette (John Larroquette)

The Celebrity Tweet Directory

Celebrity Tweets

Life is too short to waste. Dreams are fulfilled only through action, not through endless planning to take action. - D. Schwartz
@aplusk (Ashton Kutcher)

Tori Spelling
@torianddean
Followers: 87,063
Beverly Hills 90210

Blair Underwood
@BlairUnderwood
Followers: 8,326
LA Law

Brent Spiner
@BrentSpiner
Followers: 1,242,611
Star Trek: The Next Generation

Michael Urie
@michaelurie
Followers: 21,830
Ugly Betty

John Stamos
@JohnStamos
Followers: 92,966
Full House, ER

Wilmer Valderrama
@WillyVille
Followers: 8,333
That 70s Show

Chrishell Stause
@Chrishell7
Followers: 5,590
All My Children

Kate Walsh
@k8_walsh
Followers: 12,268
Grey's Anatomy, Private Practice

Anna Perez de Tagle
@AnnaMariaPdT
Followers: 57,065
Hannah Montana

Adam West
@therealadamwest
Followers: 4,853
Batman, The Family Guy

Celebrity Tweets

I miss my dead dog so much I pet his box of ashes
@margaretcho (Margaret Cho)

Aisha Tyler
@aishatyler
Followers: 10,752
Friends, The Ghost Whisperer

Wil Wheaton
@wilw
Followers: 1,491,502
Star Trek: The Next Generation

Rumer Willis
@TheRue
Followers: 107,203
90210

Adam Woodyatt
@AdamWoodyatt
Followers: 22,670
East Enders

Rainn Wilson
@rainnwilson
Followers: 1,650,715
The Office

Nick Zano
@NICKZANO
Followers: 13,590
What I Like About You

Celebrity Tweets
Figured out facebook :) I'm not a gizmologist...
@PamelaDAnderson (Pamela Anderson)

Theatre Actresses

Shoshana Bean
@shoshanabean
Followers: 5,049
Wicked

Kristin Chenoweth
@KChenoweth
Followers: 59,297
Pushing Daisies, Wicked

Celebrity Tweets
I love Stephen Colbert. Period.
@KChenoweth (Kristin Chenoweth)

Movie Directors/Producers

Wes Craven
@wescraven
Followers: 25,419
Scream 1, 2, 3

Jon Favreau
@Jon_Favreau
Followers: 559,901
Rudy, Swingers, Elf, Iron Man

The Celebrity Tweet Directory

Celebrity Tweets
Favorite thing I've heard today from a reporter: "I have nothing to Twitter about."
Perhaps the social statement of the decade.
@JasonReitman (Jason Reitman)

James Gunn
@james_gunn
Followers: 19,606
Slither, Dawn of the Dead

Tyler Perry
@tylerperry
Followers: 62,350
Madea series, Meet the Browns

David Lynch
@DAVID_LYNCH
Followers: 176,763
Blue Velvet, Mulholland Drive

Jason Reitman
@JasonReitman
Followers: 17,067
Thank You for Smoking, Juno

Frank Marshall
@LeDoctor
Followers: 5,802
The Curious Case of Benjamin Button

Eli Roth
@eliroth
Followers: 12,914
Hostel 1-2, Grindhouse

Adam McKay
@GhostPanther
Followers: 13,884
Anchorman, Talladega Nights

Kevin Smith
@ThatKevinSmith
Followers: 11,278
Clerks, Jersey Girl

Celebrity Tweets
Hunting season opens 2day in Mich. Nutty local state rep & sen have intro'd bill 2 allow
college students 2 carry handguns on campuses.
@MMFlint (Michael Moore)

Michael Moore
@MMFlint
Followers: 477,604
Roger and Me, Bowling for Columbine

Quentin J. Tarantino
@QJTarantino
Followers: 27,628
Reservoir Dogs, Kill Bill 1, 2

Celebrity Tweets
TWILIGHTers! I offer 1000 sparkly prayers for safe passage to your nearest popcorn
cathedral for this, your most holy day ever... 'til June.
@ThatKevinSmith (Kevin Smith)

Cash Warren
@cash_warren
Followers: 27,522
Independent Lens, Made in America

TV Directors/Producers

Neal Baer
@NealBaer
Followers: 4,286
Law and Order: SVU

Dan Harmon
@danharmon
Followers: 5,451
The Sarah Silverman Show, Community

Larry David
@larry_david
Followers: 98,339
Seinfeld, Curb Your Enthusiasm

Greg Yaitanes
@GregYaitanes
Followers: 96,268
House, season 6

Celebrity Tweets
So, I've been sitting here for 10 minutes. No one has said anything. Is this supposed to do something? Did I break The Twitter?
@larry_david (Larry David)

Celebrity Chefs/Foodies

Kristin Amico
@offbeat_eating
Followers: 2,223
Food critic

Allison Day
@sushiday
Followers: 1,172
Blogger

Matt Armendariz
@MattArmendariz
Followers: 2,897
Food photographer, blogger

Giada De Laurentiis
@GDeLaurentiis
Followers: 29,308
Everyday Italian, Giada at Home

Addie Broyles
@broylesa
Followers: 2,889
Food writer

Jamie and Bobby Deen
@thedeenbros
Followers: 7,107
Road Tasted

Celebrity Tweets
Is it me or do Chilaquiles qualify as inhalants?
@MattArmendariz (Matt Armendariz)

Andrea Chiu
@TOfoodie
Followers: 3,474
Restaurant reviewer, blogger

Paula Deen
@Paula_Deen
Followers: 54,652
Paula's Home Cooking

Celebrity Tweets
Time to wake up to hunger-49 Million Americans struggle with it. Join General Mills
support of @FeedingAmerica PFPChallenge.com
@roccodispirito (Rocco Dispirito)

Cat Cora
@catcora
Followers: 7,222
Iron Chef America

Rocco Dispirito
@roccodispirito
Followers: 17,269
Rocco Gets Real

Chris Cosentino
@offalchris
Followers: 5,156
Incanto

Guy Fieri
@ChefGuyFieri
Followers: 22,807
Diners, Drive-ins and Dives

Susan Filson
@StickyGooeyChef
Followers: 2,835
Food writer, cooking instructor

Sarah J. Gim
@TheDelicious
Followers: 8,255
TasteSpotting

Bobby Flay
@bflay
Followers: 36,192
Throwdown with Bobby Flay

Nadia Giosia
@bitchinkitchen
Followers: 2,568
The Bitchin Kitchen Cookbook

Celebrity Tweets
Did you know the Lollipop was named after a famous turn of the century race horse?
@Foodimentary (Foodimentary)

Tyler Florence
@TylerFlorence
Followers: 23,217
Tyler's Ultimate

Sandy Gluck
@everydayfoodsan
Followers: 1,198
Everyday Food

Celebrity Tweets
p.s. if you lover dessert & live anywhere near NYC & you have not had the Cheesecake at Chikalicious, you're missing out on transcendence.
@shunafish (Shuna Fish Lydo)

Foodimentary
@Foodimentary
Followers: 95,336
Food facts Website

Gael Greene
@GaelGreene
Followers: 7,011
Restaurant critic

Bethenny Frankel
@Bethenny
Followers: 84,137
The Apprentice: Martha Stewart

Jaden Hair
@steamykitchen
Followers: 27,996
Food writer, photographer

Brian J. Geiger
@thefoodgeek
Followers: 2,939
Fine Cooking, thefoodgeek.com

Carolyn Jung
@CarolynJung
Followers: 2,445
Food/wine writer

The Celebrity Tweet Directory

Celebrity Tweets
Saw gorgeous rainbow today, ascending from Tiburon. No surprise- plenty of pots of gold there.
@dcpatterson (Daniel Patterson)

Julie Kalivretenos
@JulieK
Followers: 1,585
Food writer, gourmet

Cybele May
@candyblog
Followers: 2,184
Blogger

Emeril Lagasse
@Emeril
Followers: 31,856
Emeril Live

Aaron McCargo Jr.
@ChefMcCargo
Followers: 952
Big Daddy's House

Celebrity Tweets
Strolling up Broadway. Fifty degrees in December! Gray's Papaya: Crsip bun, nappy dog, sweet onions. Mustard on my fingers. I am happy.
@ruthreichl (Ruth Reichl)

Ed Levine
@edlevine
Followers: 4,041
Food writer, blogger

Patrick and Gina Neely
@the_neelys
Followers: 5,684
Down Home with the Neelys

Shuna Fish Lydo
@shunafish
Followers: 2,658
Pastry chef, writer

Jamie Oliver
@jamie_oliver
Followers: 240,719
The Naked Chef

Marc Matsumoto
@norecipes
Followers: 2,201
Food writer, photographer

Cate O'Malley
@CateOMalley
Followers: 2,023
Food writer

Celebrity Tweets
Y'all, I'm on @leolaporte list of foodies, my geeks tell me this is a big deal, so, thank you Leo.
@Paula_Deen (Paula Deen)

Celebrity Chefs/Foodies

Karen Page
@**KarenAndAndrew**
Followers: 1,534
The Flavor Bible

Daniel Patterson
@**dcpatterson**
Followers: 1,654
Coi

Wolfgang Puck
@**WolfgangBuzz**
Followers: 1,572
Spago

Rachael Ray
@**RachaelRayShow**
Followers: 19,075
30 Minute Meals, Rachael Ray

Ruth Reichl
@**ruthreichl**
Followers: 23,049
Gourmet Magazine

Michael Ruhlman
@**ruhlman**
Followers: 7,984
Chef, food writer, blogger

Mark Tafoya
@**ChefMark**
Followers: 7,089
Culinary Media Network

Herschell Taghap
@**SpecialDark**
Followers: 1,050
Chef, blogger

Pim Té
@**chezpim**
Followers: 5,257
The Foodie Handbook

Robb Walsh
@**robbwalsh**
Followers: 1,780
The Tex-Mex Cookbook

Andrew Zimmern
@**andrewzimmern**
Followers: 10,791
Bizarre Foods

The Celebrity Tweet Directory

Comedians

Stephen Colbert
@StephenAtHome
Followers: 1,221,099
The Colbert Report

Jimmy Fallon
@jimmyfallon
Followers: 2,249,605
Late Night with Jimmy Fallon

Dane Cook
@danecook
Followers: 1,331,550
My Best Friend's Girl, Good Luck Chuck

Craig Ferguson
@LateLateShowHos
Followers: 12,920
The Late Late Show

Bill Cosby
@BillCosby
Followers: 673,932
The Cosby Show

Stephen Fry
@stephenfry
Followers: 1,025,048
V for Vendetta, Bones

Celebrity Tweets
ive about had it with the kardashians. they are like fake people. is anything real going on there?
@davidspade (David Spade)

Dan Cummins
@D_Cummins
Followers: 1,255
Comedy Central Presents

Dave Gorman
@DaveGorman
Followers: 57,405
Are You Dave Gorman?

Ellen DeGeneres
@TheEllenShow
Followers: 3,763,912
The Ellen DeGeneres Show

Dana Gould
@DanaJGould
Followers: 4,204
The Simpsons writer, The Aristocrats

Andy Dick
@andydick
Followers: 46,971
Road Trip

Kathy Griffin
@kathygriffin
Followers: 211,183
My Life on the D List

Bill Engvall
@billengvall
Followers: 17,781
The Bill Engvall Show

Ian Harvie
@ianharvie
Followers: 872
The Ian Harvie Show

Comedians

John Heffron

@JohnHeffron

Followers: 5,754

Last Comic Standing

Penn Jillette

@pennjillette

Followers: 1,478,239

Penn & Teller

Pee-wee Herman

@peeweeherman

Followers: 229,223

Pee-Wee's Playhouse, Pushing Daisies

Jamie Kennedy

@jamiekennedy

Followers: 45,426

The Jamie Kennedy Experiment

Richard Herring

@Herring1967

Followers: 19,731

Lee and Herring

C.K. Louis

@cklouis

Followers: 48,180

Chewed Up, Hilarious

Eddie Ifft

@eddieifft

Followers: 1,453

Comedy Central Presents

Bill Maher

@billmaher

Followers: 73,895

Real Time with Bill Maher

Tim Minchin
@**timminchin**
Followers: 45,975
Tim Minchin and Friends

Paula Poundstone
@**paulapoundstone**
Followers: 20,329
Wait Wait…Don't Tell Me!

Tracy Morgan
@**RealTracyMorgan**
Followers: 74,012
Saturday Night Live, 30 Rock

Rob Riggle
@**RobRiggle**
Followers: 923,330
The Daily Show

Chris Moyles
@**CHRISM0YLES**
Followers: 7,897
The Chris Moyles Show

Chris Rock
@**ImChrisRock**
Followers: 10,474
Comedy Central Presents

Celebrity Tweets
A grandchild is God punishing your children for what they did to you.
@**BillCosby (Bill Cosby)**

Kevin Nealon
@**kevin_nealon**
Followers: 1,060,537
Saturday Night Live, Weeds

Joe Rogan
@**joerogandotnet**
Followers: 76,411
News Radio, Fear Factor

Celebrity Tweets
Wouldn't you guys want to see Simon Cowell kiss Susan Boyle when she wins Britain's Got Talent? Best thing on TV since Magnum P.I.
@**LateLateShowHos (Craig Ferguson)**

Dara O'Briain
@**daraobriain**
Followers: 64,119
Mock the Week

Bob Saget
@**bobsaget**
Followers: 5,121,212
Full House, America's Funniest Home Videos

Celebrity Tweets
My Wife and Son talking at the doctor's office -"Z, do you want to be a doctor?" No."
"Why not?" "All these sick guys, it's not my problem."
@**Pennjillette (Penn Jillette)**

Comedians

Adam Sandler
@adamsandler
Followers: 205,688
Saturday Night Live, Happy Gilmore

David Spade
@davidspade
Followers: 184,584
Saturday Night Live, Tommy Boy

Celebrity Tweets
I like to 'dog ear' my cat's ear. Yes, it does create an identity crisis but it helps me remember where I left off with him.
@kevin_nealon (Kevin Nealon)

Jerry Seinfeld
@jerry_seinfeld
Followers: 16,450
Seinfeld

Nick Thune
@nickthune
Followers: 7,132
Comedy Central Presents

Celebrity Tweets
No more complaining about Kanye. Did you expect him NOT to cause a scene? You don't go to a movie and get surprised when the lights go off
@jerry_seinfeld (Jerry Seinfeld)

Dax Shepard
@daxshepard1
Followers: 13,578
Punk'd

Paul F. Tompkins
@PFTompkins
Followers: 29,223
The Daily Show

Michael Showalter
@mshowalter
Followers: 38,847
Michael & Michael Have Issues

Daniel Tosh
@danieltosh
Followers: 82,311
Tosh 2.0

Celebrity Tweets
Obama slipped Chinese President a fiver, and said, "We owe you $600 billion, but I just want to give you something each month."
@paulapundstone (Paula Poundstone)

Sarah Silverman
@SarahKSilverman
Followers: 357,699
The Sarah Silverman Program

Shawn Wayans
@Shawn_Wayans
Followers: 5,935
In Living Color, The Wayans Bros

The Celebrity Tweet Directory

Celebrity Tweets
Big realization: Pepperidge Farm remembers. They really do. What they remember? I'm not sure. But I know they remember.
@mshowalter (Michael Showalter)

Lizz Winstead
@lizzwinstead
Followers: 3,454
Co-creator, The Daily Show

Journalists

PRESS

The Celebrity Tweet Directory

Dan Abrams
@danielabrams
Followers: 6,251
NBC Chief Legal Analyst

Jonathan Alter
@jonathanalter
Followers: 714
Newsweek, MSNBC Analyst

Mika Brzezinski
@morningmika
Followers: 14,510
Morning Joe

Anderson Cooper
@andersoncooper
Followers: 369,907
Anderson Cooper 360

Celebrity Tweets
They're amazing, walls. They hold up the roof, but they're also handy for hanging pictures. I like that.
@Andy_Rooney (Andy Rooney)

Christiane Amanpour
@AmanpourCNN
Followers: 12,181
Amanpour

Bret Baier
@SpecialReport
Followers: 102,323
Special Report

Matt Cooper
@mattizcoop
Followers: 3,208
Time Magazine

Katie Couric
@katiecouric
Followers: 54,447
CBS Evening News

Celebrity Tweets
I am struggling to justify my membership in the latest mass communication cult.
@Morleysafer (Morley Safer)

Contessa Brewer
@contessabrewer
Followers: 9,881
MSNBC

Campbell Brown
@CNNCampbell
Followers: 1,863
Cambell Brown

Chris Cuomo
@ChrisCuomo
Followers: 872,247
Good Morning America

Ann Curry
@AnnCurry
Followers: 857,421
The Today Show, Dateline

Journalists

Lou Dobbs
@loudobbsnews
Followers: 7,029
Lou Dobbs Tonight

Nancy Grace
@theNancyGrace
Followers: 6,750
Nancy Grace

John Donvan
@JohnDonvanNL
Followers: 1,252,065
ABC News

Dr. Sanjay Gupta
@sanjayguptaCNN
Followers: 1,025,302
CNN Chief Medical Correspondent

Susan Filan
@attysusanfilan
Followers: 293
MSNBC Senior Legal Analyst

Tamron Hall
@tamronhall
Followers: 10,713
MSNBC Anchor

Sasha Frere-Jones
@sfj
Followers: 9,701
The New Yorker

Chris Hansen
@chrishansen
Followers: 11,880
To Catch a Predator

Willie Geist
@WillieGeist1
Followers: 8,108
Way Too Early with Willie Geist

Tony Harris
@TonyHarrisCNN
Followers: 747
CNN

The Celebrity Tweet Directory

Marlon Jackson: "Maybe now Michael they will leave you alone."
@latimesharriet (Harriet Ryan)

Lester Holt
@LesterHoltNBC
Followers: 21
NBC Nightly News, The Today Show

Don Lemon
@donlemoncnn
Followers: 60,921
CNN

Arianna Huffington
@ariannahuff
Followers: 204,308
The Huffington Post

Rachel Maddow
@maddow
Followers: 1,470,746
Rachel Maddow Show

Larry King
@kingsthings
Followers: 1,428,697
Larry King Live

Cynthia McFadden
@CynthiaMcFadden
Followers: 6,397
Nightline

Hoda Kotb
@hodakotb
Followers: 20,942
The Today's Show, Dateline NBC

Maria Menounos
@mariamenounos
Followers: 24,099
Access Hollywood, The Today Show

Celebrity Tweets
She says the SEC should have been looking at Madoff not her. My exclusive with the ever- fascinating Martha Stewart tonight on Nightline
CynthiaMcFadden (@Cynthia McFadden)

Paul Krugman
@NYTimeskrugman
Followers: 177,520
Economist, The New York Times

Terry Moran
@TerryMoran
Followers: 1,275,184
Nightline

Celebrity Tweets
Costas' turtleneck is quite regal.
@RussertXM_NBC (Luke Russert)

Journalists

Peggy Noonan
@Peggynoonannyc
Followers: 4,840
The Wall Street Journal

Al Roker
@alroker
Followers: 45,716
The Today Show

Celebrity Tweets
Nutty is nutty, trash it all Fox.
@TonyHarrisCNN (Tony Harris)

Kyra Phillips
@KyraCNN
Followers: 6,509
CNN Newsroom

Andy Rooney
@Andy__Rooney
Followers: 8,929
60 Minutes

Byron Pitts
@byronpitts
Followers: 1,786
CBS Evening News, 60 Minutes

Charlie Rose
@charlierose
Followers: 1,692
Charlie Rose

Celebrity Tweets
How soon until the "Larry, You're Being Inappropriate" ironic t-shirts hit the web? Have
I mentioned I'm on page 70 of Carrie's book? I am.
@WillieGeist1 (Willie Geist)

Dylan Ratigan
@DylanRatigan
Followers: 5,051
Morning Meeting with Dylan Ratigan

Luke Russert
@RussertXM_NBC
Followers: 6,777
60/20 Sports

Eugene Robinson
@Eugene_Robinson
Followers: 1,522
The Washington Post, MSNBC, author

Harriet Ryan
@latimesharriet
Followers: 647
Los Angeles Times

Celebrity Tweets
so tonight I interview Elmo. Yes...that Elmo. Red. Furry. It's why I went into journalism.
It's on @nightline.
@JohnDonvanNL (John Donvan)

Morley Safer
@morleysafer
Followers: 20
60 Minutes

Maria Shriver
@mariashriver
Followers: 278,515
First Lady of California

Rick Sanchez
@ricksanchezcnn
Followers: 115,850
CNN

David Shuster
@DavidShuster
Followers: 22,626
MSNBC

 Celebrity Tweets
"Our true home is in the present moment."-Thich Nhat Hanh
@AnnCurry (Anne Curry)

Joe Scarborough
@JoeNBC
Followers: 25,121
Morning Joe

Harry Smith
@earlyshowharry
Followers: 3,887
The Early Show

Ed Schultz
@edshow
Followers: 157
The Ed Show

Dr. Nancy Snyderman
@DrNancyMSNBC
Followers: 2,352
NBC News Chief Medical Editor, Dr. Nancy

 Celebrity Tweets
I'm with Sarah Palin. A picture of her taken for a running magazine on Newsweek's
cover for a political piece? Not fair.
@contessabrewer (Contessa Brewer)

Steve Sebelius
@SteveSebelius
Followers: 427
CityLife

Greta Van Susteren
@gretawire
Followers: 25,226
On The Record

 Celebrity Tweets
see husband's investigation on mystery of middle eastern men getting married in
small NY town just before 9/11
@morningmika (Mika Brzezinski)

Joan Walsh
@joanwalsh
Followers: 8,187
Salon.com

Robert Woodruff
@BobWoodruff
Followers: 9,993
Focus Earth with Bob Woodruff

Barbara Walters
@BarbaraJWalters
Followers: 495,016
The View

Jenna Wortham
@jennydeluxe
Followers: 169,773
The New York Times

Celebrity Tweets
I had a Rwandan guest on today who doesn't believe in the reconciliation process there – says the fire is still burning under the ashes
@AmanourCNN (Christiane Amanpur)

Richard Wolffe
@richardwolffedc
Followers: 910
Author, MSNBC

Toby Young
@toadmeister
Followers: 7,845
How to Lose Friends and Alienate People

Celebrity Tweets
PO or bust folks don't even know that Howard Dean's proposal in 2004 had no public option. The idea wasn't even invented til 2005.
@jonathaqnalter (Jonathan Alter)

Music

311
@311
Followers: 15,207
Alternative rock band

30 Seconds To Mars
@14azar
Followers: 78
Alternative rock band

A Rocket To The Moon
@we_are_arttm
Followers: 13,376
Alternative rock band

Paula Abdul
@PaulaAbdul
Followers: 1,424,133
Singer, producer, dancer, choreographer

Lily Allen
@lilyroseallen
Followers: 1,774,804
Singer

Kris Allen
@KrisAllen
Followers: 121,729
Singer, songwriter

Amerie
@itsmeAmerie
Followers: 66,491
Singer, songwriter

Anberlin
@anberlin
Followers: 23,875
Alternative rock band

Celebrity Tweets
If you must judge; First improve yourself, and then judge others.
llcoolj (LL Cool J)

Bryan Adams
@bryanadams
Followers: 15,324
Singer, songwriter, photographer

William Adams Jr.
@iamwill
Followers: 114,503
Black Eyed Peas

Marvin Lee Aday
@RealMeatLoaf
Followers: 8,221
Singer

Peter Andre
@MrPeterAndre
Followers: 374,856
Singer, songwriter

David Archuleta
@DavidArchie
Followers: 274,726
Singer, songwriter

Monica Arnold
@MonicaMyLife
Followers: 135,715
Singer, songwriter

Music

A-Trak
@atrak
Followers: 36,070
DJ

Beastie Boys
@beastieboys
Followers: 39,048
Rock/rap/hip hop band

B Real
@B_Real420
Followers: 21,056
Rapper, Cypress Hill

Jona Bechtolt
@teamyacht
Followers: 2,974
Musician, The Blow

Sebastian Bach
@sebastianbach
Followers: 23,192
Singer, Skid Row, actor

Beck
@beck
Followers: 6,226
Singer, songwriter, musician

Erykah Badu
@fatbellybella
Followers: 70,030
Singer, songwriter

Natasha Bedingfield
@natashabdnfield
Followers: 3,135
Singer, songwriter

Sara Bareilles
@SaraBareilles
Followers: 1,670,601
Singer, songwriter, pianist

Adrian Belew
@THEadrianbelew
Followers: 593
Singer, songwriter, guitarist, King Crimson

Celebrity Tweets
Every time I break through and the song starts flowing out- every time this year- I stop the music and realize is raining again...
@AmyLeeEV (Amy Lee)

Barenaked Ladies
@barenakedladies
Followers: 8,270
Rock band

Justin Bieber
@justinbieber
Followers: 535,948
Singer

Travis Barker
@trvsbrkr
Followers: 329,264
Drummer, blink-182

Andrew Bird
@andrewbird
Followers: 16,031
Singer

The Celebrity Tweet Directory

Mary J Blige
@maryjblige
Followers: 378,483
Singer, songwriter, producer, actress

Toni Braxton
@tonibraxton
Followers: 19,527
Singer, songwriter

Wes Borland
@wesborland
Followers: 16,552
Guitarist, Limp Bizkit

Christopher Bridges
@ludajuice
Followers: 260,770
Rapper, actor

Celebrity Tweets
If you have passion and drive to do something, nothing will be able to get in your way of accomplishing that goal.. XoP
@PaulaAbdul (Paula Abdul)

blink-182
@blink182
Followers: 58,738
Rock band

Calvin Cordozar Broadus
@snoopdogg
Followers: 694,575
Rapper, producer, actor

Blitzen Trapper
@BlitzenTrapper
Followers: 5,334
Folk band

Cary Brothers
@carybrothers
Followers: 4,543
Singer, songwriter

Michelle Branch
@michellebranch
Followers: 48,844
Singer, songwriter, guitarist

Melanie Brown
@OfficialMelB
Followers: 36,218
Singer, Spice Girls

Paul Brandt
@paulbrandt
Followers: 2,769
Singer, songwriter

Jimmy Buffett
@jimmybuffett
Followers: 186,635
Singer, songwriter, author

Celebrity Tweets
Just saw the documentary film The Cove, about Japanese fishermen who slaughter dolphins for a living, it's shameful. Please stop the killing
@bryanadams (Bryan Adams)

Music

Alexandra Burke
@alexandramusic
Followers: 70,899
Singer

Chris Carrabba
@ChrisCarrabba
Followers: 18,726
Singer, guitarist, Dashboard Confessional

Stanley Burrell
@MCHammer
Followers: 1,674,123
Rapper, entertainer, dancer

Kenny Chesney
@kennychesney
Followers: 205,667
Singer, guitarist

Kandi Burruss
@KandiConnection
Followers: 135,063
Singer, songwriter, producer

Kelly Clarkson
@theclarksonk
Followers: 1,200
Singer, songwriter

Ryan Cabrera
@ryan_cabrera
Followers: 13,988
Singer

George Clinton
@george_clinton
Followers: 4,741
Singer, songwriter, producer

Mariah Carey
@MariahCarey
Followers: 2,002,428
Singer, songwriter, producer, actress

Anita Cochran
@anitacochran
Followers: 1,395
Singer, songwriter, guitarist, producer

Celebrity Tweets
I'm four songs into the new record. I have a stomach ache from how happy i am. Apparently happy feels like bad sushi. Sigh.
@SaraBareilles (Sara Bareilles)

Vanessa Carlton
@VanessaCarlton
Followers: 4,911
Singer, songwriter, pianist

Sean John Combs
@iamdiddy
Followers: 2,269,522
Rapper, producer, actor, designer

Celebrity Tweets
We all have something to celebrate, life, so that makes you a celebrity! Everybody is a star!
@maryjblige (Mary J Blige)

Coldplay
@coldplay
Followers: 2,269,759
Alternative rock band

Jamie Cullum
@jamiecullum
Followers: 26,284
Singer, songwriter, musician

Collective Soul
@collective_soul
Followers: 27,929
Alternative rock band

Rivers Cuomo
@riverscuomo
Followers: 2,074
Singer, songwriter, guitarist, Weezer

David Cook
@thedavidcook
Followers: 75,076
Singer, songwriter

Billy Ray Cyrus
@billyraycyrus
Followers: 320,713
Singer, songwriter, actor

Billy Corgan
@Billy
Followers: 28,648
Singer, The Smashing Pumpkins

Trace Cyrus
@TraceCyrus
Followers: 337,675
Singer, songwriter, guitarist

Chris Cornell
@chriscornell
Followers: 1,279,874
Singer, songwriter, Soundgarden, Audioslave

Chris Daughtry
@CHRIS_Daughtry
Followers: 108,896
Singer, songwriter, guitarist, Daughtry

Celebrity Tweets
It's a bit awkward sitting on a plane next to someone who is reading a magazine article about you but they're clueless it's you next to them
@michellebranch (Michelle Branch)

Jonathan Coulton
@jonathancoulton
Followers: 39,250
Singer, songwriter

Taylor Dayne
@taylor_dayne
Followers: 7,041
Singer, actress

Counting Crows
@countingcrows
Followers: 1,044,443
Alternative rock band

Death Cab for Cutie
@dcfctours
Followers: 9,997
Alternative rock band

Music

Kristinia DeBarge
@Kristinia
Followers: 25,472
Singer, songwriter

Alex DeLeon
@alexanderdeleon
Followers: 20,110
Singer, The Cab

Depeche Mode
@depechemode
Followers: 249,594
Alternative rock band

Jason Derulo
@jasonderulo
Followers: 9,626
Singer, songwriter, choreographer, producer

Neil Diamond
@NeilDiamond
Followers: 31,108
Singer, songwriter, musician

Bentley Dierks
@DierksBentley
Followers: 49,341
Singer

Ani Difranco
@anidifranco
Followers: 11,049
Singer, songwriter, guitarist

Dixie Chicks
@dixiechicks
Followers: 227,601
Country rock band

Fred Durst
@freddurst
Followers: 1,400,863
Singer, Limp Bizkit

Garrett Dutton III
@glove
Followers: 7,572
Singer, G. Love & Special Sauce

Fabulous
@myfabolouslife
Followers: 361,517
Rapper, songwriter

Fall Out Boy
@falloutboy
Followers: 116,445
Rock band

Perry Farrell
@perryfarrell
Followers: 12,772
Singer, Jane's Addiction

Stacy Ann Ferguson
@Fergie
Followers: 39,315
Singer, songwriter, Black Eyed Peas

Celebrity Tweets
The album "lost souls" by the doves is top 3 fav record ever.
@VanessaCarlton (Vanessa Carlton)

The Celebrity Tweet Directory

Celebrity Tweets
The human heart is like a broken clock that keeps working.
@Billy (Billy Corgan)

Lupe Fiasco
@wearelasers
Followers: 38,727
Singer

Michael Franti
@michaelfranti
Followers: 7,371
Singer, songwriter, Michael Franti & Spearhead

Dan Finnerty
@thedanband
Followers: 2,546
Singer

Adam Freeland
@Adam_Freeland
Followers: 4,277
DJ, producer

Wale Folarin
@wale
Followers: 127,110
Singer

Alex Greenwald
@ALECKSU
Followers: 6,315
Singer, Phantom Planet

Benjamin Folds
@BenjaminFolds
Followers: 26,790
Singer, songwriter, musician, Ben Folds

Bjork Guomundsdottir
@bjork
Followers: 63,381
Singer, songwriter, producer, actress

Celebrity Tweets
Some mornings I wake up to "signs" telling me to make changes and to think differently. These are the mornings that impress me the most.
@freddurst (Fred Durst)

Farrah Franklin
@FarrahFranklin
Followers: 20,422
Singer, actress, model

Richard Melvin Hall
@thelittleidiot
Followers: 1,038,960
Singer, songwriter, DJ

Celebrity Tweets
People really like to twist words on news...Wow seriously!
@Fergie (Fergie)

Music

Nelly Furtado
@NellyFurtado
Followers: 298,336
Singer, songwriter, producer, actress

Amy Grant
@amygrant
Followers: 17,221
Singer, songwriter, guitarist

Stephani Germanotta
@ladygaga
Followers: 1,653,323
Singer, songwriter

Josh Groban
@joshgroban
Followers: 98,532
Singer, songwriter, musician, actor

Deborah Gibson
@DeborahGibson
Followers: 19,005
Singer, songwriter

Brett Gurewitz
@OblivionPact
Followers: 6,950
Songwriter, guitarist, Bad Religion

Aaron Gillespie
@aaronrgillespie
Followers: 21,000
Singer, The Almost

Calvin Harris
@calvinharris
Followers: 149,957
Singer, songwriter, producer

Danny Gokey
dannygokey
Followers: 104,352
Singer

Mya Harris
@MISSMYA
Followers: 89,262
Singer, songwriter, producer, actress

Celebrity Tweets
I never thought I would be able to say this…but by not having a single tattoo I'm really sticking it to conformity.
@joshgroban (Josh Groban)

Goo Goo Dolls
@googoodolls
Followers: 9,251
Alternative rock band

Ciara Harris
@ciara
Followers: 262,609
Singer, producer, dancer

Alex Gopher
@alexgopher
Followers: 1,212
Singer

Imogen Heap
@imogenheap
Followers: 1,284,196
Singer, songwriter

The Celebrity Tweet Directory

Celebrity Tweets
The freaks are out in full force tonight, I love Hollyweird!
@SlashHudson (Slash)

Hawthorne Heights
@HawthorneHgts
Followers: 3,251
Rock band

Mandisa Hundley
@mandisaofficial
Followers: 9,896
Singer

Faith Hill
@FaithHill
Followers: 31,371
Singer

Enrique Iglesias
@enrique305
Followers: 25,473
Singer, songwriter, actor

Keri Hilson
@MissKeriBaby
Followers: 431,629
Singer, The Clutch

Curtis Jackson III
@50cent
Followers: 1,973,469
Rapper

Mark Hoppus
@markhoppus
Followers: 1,468,419
Singer, blink-182/+44

Janet Jackson
@JanetJackson
Followers: 436,855
Singer

Julianne Hough
@juliannehough
Followers: 74,747
Singer

Jamey Jasta
@jameyjasta
Followers: 7,619
Singer, Kingdom of Sorrow

Celebrity Tweets
I hate waking up when its raining
@Enrique305 (Enrique Iglesias)

Slash Hudson
@SlashHudson
Followers: 114,409
Guitarist, Guns N' Roses

Wyclef Jean
@wyclef
Followers: 1,150,690
Rapper, producer

Joan Jet
@joanjett
Followers: 5,868
Singer, songwriter, guitarist, producer

Alicia Keys
@aliciakeys
Followers: 539,152
Singer, pianist, actress

Michael Johns
@michael_johns
Followers: 10,063
Singer, songwriter

Solange Knowles
@solangeknowles
Followers: 342,615
Singer, songwriter, actress

Celebrity Tweets
I love you, Mike, and I miss you. Dunk.
@JanetJackson (Janet Jackson)

Alvin Nathanial Joiner
@mrxtothaz
Followers: 32,182
Rapper, actor, TV personality

Jewel Kilcher
@jeweljk
Followers: 61,336
Singer, songwriter, guitarist, poet

Kimberly Jones
@lilkimsworld
Followers: 27,930
Rapper, Junior M.A.F.I.A.

Sean Kingston
@seankingston
Followers: 142,669
Singer, rapper

Celebrity Tweets
All hail freedom of expression and artistic integrity. :) fans: I adore u.
@adamlambert (Adam Lambert)

Jonas Brothers
@Jonasbrothers
Followers: 1,083,878
Singers, songwriters, musicians

Andreas Kleerup
@kleerup
Followers: 1,799
Drummer, The Meat Boys, producer

Zoe Keating
@zoecello
Followers: 1,253,175
Cellist

Jonathan Knight
@JonathanRKnight
Followers: 57,302
Singer, New Kids on the Block

The Celebrity Tweet Directory

Jordan Knight
@jordanknight
Followers: 56,611
Singer, New Kids on the Block

John Legend
@johnlegend
Followers: 1,506,292
Singer, actor

Lenny Kravitz
@LennyKravitz
Followers: 1,422,113
Singer, songwriter, musician, producer, actor

Sean Ono Lennon
@seanonolennon
Followers: 8,199
Singer, songwriter, actor

Ben Kweller
@benkweller
Followers: 13,070
Singer, songwriter, musician

Alex Lloyd
@alexlloydmusic
Followers: 215
Singer, songwriter

Adam Lambert
@adamlambert
Followers: 239,047
Singer, songwriter

Lisa Loeb
@lisaloeb4real
Followers: 16,740
Singer, songwriter

Celebrity Tweets
"You are the average of the five people you spend the most time with." - Jim Rohn
@aliciakeys (Alicia Keys)

Queen Latifah
@IAMQUEENLATIFAH
Followers: 260,225
Singer, rapper, actress

Kenny Loggins
@kennyloggins
Followers: 3,902
Singer, songwriter, musician

Amy Lee
@AmyLeeEV
Followers: 22,203
Singer, Evanescence

Jennifer Lopez
@JLo
Followers: 71,740
Singer, producer, dancer, actress

Celebrity Tweets
You would have an easier time finding the arc of the covenant in mint condition, than a stick of deodorant in Japan. Not much sweating here.
@seanonolennon (Sean Lennon)

52

Music

Lonnie Lynn Jr.
@common
Followers: 129,414
Rapper, actor

John Mayer
@johncmayer
Followers: 2,649,750
Singer, songwriter, guitarist

Joel Madden
@JoelMadden
Followers: 311,278
Singer, Good Charlotte

Martina McBride
@martinamcbride
Followers: 50,330
Singer, songwriter

Celebrity Tweets
Cool. My song, "Let's Forget About It" is on at IKEA!
@lisaloeb4real (Lisa Loeb)

Tracy Marrow
@FINALLEVEL
Followers: 27,140
Rapper, actor, author

Paul McCartney
@PaulMcCartney
Followers: 24,711
Singer, songwriter, The Beatles/Wings

Ricky Martin
@ricky_martin
Followers: 449,202
Singer

Jesse McCartney
@JesseMcCartney
Followers: 139,529
Singer, songwriter, actor

Marshall Mathers
@Eminem
Followers: 368,514
Rapper, producer, actor

Reba McEntire
@reba
Followers: 69,185
Singer, songwriter, actress

Dave Matthews
@DaveJMatthews
Followers: 824,723
Singer, songwriter, The Dave Matthews Band

Roger McGuinn
@RogerMcGuinn
Followers: 3,554
Singer, guitarist, The Byrds

Celebrity Tweets
Wow whoever made "Die Already" really does sound like me. But it ain't.
@Eminem (Eminem)

Joey McIntyre
@joeymcintyre
Followers: 60,308
Singer, New Kids on the Block

@LoLa Monroe
DaRealAngelLola
Followers: 41,692
Singer

Katharine McPhee
@katharinemcphee
Followers: 12,925
Singer

Alecia Moore
@Pink
Followers: 674,805
Singer, songwriter

Colin Meloy
@colinmeloy
Followers: 1,151,168
Singer, Decemberists

Mandy Moore
@TheMandyMoore
Followers: 1,644,915
Singer, songwriter, actress

Celebrity Tweets
What if everyone's Twitter picture was of them flipping the bird. Maybe for a couple days. Maybe forever. Meant well or not. Just fun no?
@DaveJMatthews (Dave Matthews)

Matthew Paul Miller
@matisyahu
Followers: 1,082,010
Singer

Alanis Morissette
@morissette
Followers: 28,428
Singer, songwriter, actress

Kylie Minogue
@kylie_minogue
Followers: 26,598
Singer, songwriter, actress

Shad Moss
@bowwow614
Followers: 263,194
Rapper, actor

Celebrity Tweets
I always feel a little ripped off when there is an episode of Dateline without Keith Morrison as the correspondent.
@davenavarro6767 (Dave Navarro)

Alison Monro
@AFineFrenzy
Followers: 1,548,041
Singer, songwriter, pianist

Jason Mraz
@jason_mraz
Followers: 440,862
Singer, songwriter

Music

Dwight Myers
@heavyd
Followers: 39,240
Rapper, Heavy D & the Boyz

Aubrey O'Dea
@AubreyODay
Followers: 164,285
Singer, songwriter, Danity Kane

Terra Naomi
@terranaomi
Followers: 4,626
Singer

Ozzy Osbourne
@OfficialOzzy
Followers: 254,935
Singer

Dave Navarro
@davenavarro6767
Followers: 50,189
Guitarist, Jane's Addiction

Emily Osment
@EmilyOsment
Followers: 399,553
Singer, songwriter

Brandy Norwood
@4everBrandy
Followers: 249,859
Singer, songwriter, producer, actress

Brad Paisley
@paisleyofficial
Followers: 80,001
Singer, songwriter

Celebrity Tweets
Grandma asked if someone's phone was going off when it was actually a violin player. Then player asked 4 requests & gma said Kissed A Girl!
@katyperry (Katy Perry)

William Raymond Norwood Jr.
@RayJ
Followers: 122,454
Singer, producer

Amanda Palmer
@amandapalmer
Followers: 220,596
Singer, The Dresden Dolls

Oasis
@oasis
Followers: 46,360
Alternative rock band

Dolly Parton
@Dolly_Parton
Followers: 303,980
Singer, songwriter, musician, actress

Celebrity Tweets
Tooooooo muchhh cofffeeeeeee!!!!!./-JJ
@Jonasbrothers (Jonas Brothers)

The Celebrity Tweet Directory

Pearl Jam
@PearlJam
Followers: 275,808
Alternative rock band

Pussycat Dolls
@pcdmusic
Followers: 5,967
Pop band

Thomas Pentz
@diplo
Followers: 41,147
Songwriter, producer

Trent Reznor
@trent_reznor
Followers: 636,278
Singer, Nine Inch Nails

Celebrity Tweets
I am going to bring some coconut cake on the plane to NY.
@smokey_robinson (Smokey Robinson)

Stephen Perkins
@stephenperkins
Followers: 4,086
Drummer, Jane's Addiction

Busta Rhymes
@BusaBusss
Followers: 134,863
Rapper, songwriter, actor

Celebrity Tweets
I have said 'i love you' to so many people tonight. I can't stop hugging people. This is magical.
@taylorswift13 (Taylor Swift)

Katy Perry
@katyperry
Followers: 1,434,933
Singer, songwriter

Leann Rimes
@leannrimes
Followers: 45,337
Singer, songwriter, actress

Kellie Pickler
@kelliepickler
Followers: 179,232
Singer

Shakira Ripoll
@shakira
Followers: 422,677
Singer, songwriter

Celebrity Tweets
catching up on MAD MEN. nothing really happens. why am i so fascinated by it?
@ThisIsRobThomas (Rob Thomas)

Music

Smokey Robinson
@smokey_robinson
Followers: 26,408
Singer, songwriter, producer

Russell Simmons
@UncleRUSH
Followers: 262,799
Def Jam

Samantha Ronson
@samantharonson
Followers: 1,354,743
Singer, songwriter, DJ

James Todd Smith
@llcoolj
Followers: 304,609
Rapper, actor

Asher Roth
@asherroth
Followers: 131,153
Rapper

Shaffer Chimere Smith
@NeYoCompound
Followers: 160,445
Singer, songwriter, producer, actor

Celebrity Tweets
Is it possible that I've been going through my "terrible twos" for the past 28 years?
@Petewentz (Pete Wentz)

Kelly Rowland
@KELLY__ROWLAND
Followers: 181,662
Singer

Jordin Sparks
@TheRealJordin
Followers: 397,054
Singer, songwriter

Celebrity Tweets
Holy toledo mudhens!!!.....lou holtz just spit the word "b*tch" on espn's college football final!....amazing
@Elliottyamin (Elliott Yamin)

Paulina Rubio
@paurubio
Followers: 55,753
Singer, actress

Britney Spears
@britneyspears
Followers: 3,835,866
Singer

Gene Simmons
@genesimmons
Followers: 47,196
Singer, guitarist, Kiss

Bruce Springsteen
@springsteen
Followers: 15,100
Singer, songwriter, musician

The Celebrity Tweet Directory

Ruben Studdard
@RubenStuddard
Followers: 4,242
Singer

Justin Timberlake
@jtimberlake
Followers: 1,196,337
Singer, songwriter, actor

Celebrity Tweets
Don't be distracted by criticism. Remember-the only taste of success some people have when they take a bite out of you.~Zig Ziglar
@Ludajuice (Ludacris)

Taylor Swift
@taylorswift13
Followers: 1,907,553
Singer, songwriter, guitarist, actress

David Usher
@davidusher
Followers: 2,668
Singer, songwriter, Moist

Robin Thicke
@robinthicke
Followers: 22,788
Singer, songwriter

Raymond Usher
@UsherRaymondIV
Followers: 145,606
Singer, songwriter

Celebrity Tweets
Seems as though my twitter was hacked yesterday. I could be angry, except I secretly love how psychotically smart my fans are.
@Ladygaga (Lady Gaga)

Rob Thomas
@ThisIsRobThomas
Followers: 127,185
Singer, Matchbox Twenty

Kate Voegele
@katevoegele
Followers: 37,484
Singer, songwriter

Ahmir Thompson
@questlove
Followers: 1,118,191
Drummer, The Roots

Donnie Wahlberg
@DonnieWahlberg
Followers: 97,981
Singer, New Kids on the Block

Celebrity Tweets
I suppose its ironic that I'm giving directions to a chinese taxi driver who is lost in chinatown, what with me being a dirty gaijin.
@Thelittleidiot (Moby)

Music

Jody Watley
@jodywatley
Followers: 10,505
Singer, songwriter, producer

Amy Winehouse
@amywinehouse
Followers: 35,409
Singer, songwriter

Pete Wentz
@petewentz
Followers: 1,753,261
Guitarist, Fall Out Boy

Danny Wood
@dannywood
Followers: 38,848
Singer, New Kids on the Block

DJ WhooKid
@DJWhooKid
Followers: 35,246
DJ

Elliott Yamin
@elliottyamin
Followers: 8,680
Singer

Celebrity Tweets
they got homer simpsons voice on a GPS! homer simpson?!? Tha Boss coulda done that ishh better, and ya do know that!!
@Snoopdogg (Snoop Dogg)

Robbie Williams
@robbiewilliams
Followers: 33,649
Singer

Al Yankovic
@alyankovic
Followers: 1,462,733
Singer, songwriter, producer

Allee Willis
@AlleeWillis
Followers: 505
Songwriter

Trisha Yearwood
@TYcom
Followers: 6,482
Singer, actress

Celebrity Tweets
i just made a twitter account because it isnt cool for someone to blame you and blast you with lies...
@iamwill (will.i.am)

Patrick Wilson
@patrick_wilson
Followers: 8,438
Drummer, Weezer

Pete Yorn
@peteyorn
Followers: 1,091,934
Singer, songwriter, guitarist

The Celebrity Tweet Directory

Personalities

Rania Al Abdullah
@QueenRania
Followers: 1,061,655
Wife of King Abdullah II of Jordan

Jillian Barberie
@askjillian
Followers: 34,224
Good Day LA, Fox NFL Sunday

Alex Albrecht
@alexalbrecht
Followers: 69,016
Podcast host, The Screen Savers

Victoria Beckham
@REALVicBeckham
Followers: 25,950
The Spice Girls

Buzz Aldrin
@therealBuzz
Followers: 698,537
Astronaut

Joy Behar
@JoyVBehar
Followers: 138,342
The View

Criss Angel
@crissangel
Followers: 233,765
Mindfreak

Greg Behrendt
@gregbehrendt
Followers: 5,178
He's Just Not That Into You

Celebrity Tweets
Don't reinforce or encourage fearful or aggressive state of mind. Save affection for when your dog is calm!
@cesarmillan (Cesar Millan)

Michael Ausiello
@EWAusielloFiles
Followers: 975,663
Entertainment Weekly

Pope Benedict XVI
@Pope_Benedict
Followers: 3,157
Reigning Pope

Mark Ballas
@OfficialMBallas
Followers: 25,096
Dancing with the Stars

Tom Bergeron
@Tom_Bergeron
Followers: 10,172
Dancing with the Stars host

Tyra Banks
@tyrabanks
Followers: 634,548
Model, The Tyra Banks Show

Larry Birkhead
@larrybirkhead
Followers: 2,430
Photographer

David Blaine
@davidblaine
Followers: 254,169
Magician

Sylvia Browne
@Sylvia_Browne
Followers: 12,548
Spiritual teacher, psychic

Celebrity Tweets
Anyone notice the World Series players wearing these necklaces? Or believe they boost energy?
@DrOz (Dr. Mehmet Oz)

Lo Bosworth
@LoBosworth
Followers: 286,336
Laguna Beach, The Hills

Warren Buffett
@W_Buffett
Followers: 21,783
Investor, businessman, philanthropist

Adam Bouska
@bouska
Followers: 9,158
Photographer, Co-Founder of NO H8

Brooke Burke
@brookeburke
Followers: 1,598,624
Model, Dancing with the Stars

Celebrity Tweets
OK, I doused myself with gasoline and got out the matches. But I'm not lighting one, because I just realized Oprah's probably gonna be OK!
@marklisanti (Mark Lisanti)

Richard Branson
@richardbranson
Followers: 196,399
The Virgin Group

Billy Bush
@BillyBush
Followers: 31,271
Access Hollywood

Derren Brown
@DerrenBrown
Followers: 251,920
Magician

Adam Carolla
@adamcarolla
Followers: 60,249
The Adam Carolla Podcast

Celebrity Tweets
John use to say "I love you" every day. I didn't understand then, how lucky I was.
@yokoono (Yoko Ono)

The Celebrity Tweet Directory

Duane Dog Chapman
@DogBountyHunter
Followers: 22,404
Dog the Bounty Hunter

Adrianne Curry
@AdrianneCurry
Followers: 54,733
America's Next Top Model

Alexa Chung
@alexa_chung
Followers: 94,912
It's On with Alexa Chung

Carson Daly
@carsonjdaly
Followers: 39,464
Last Call with Carson Daly

Jean-Michel Cousteau
@JMCousteau
Followers: 1,647
French explorer

Donny Deutsch
@Donny_Deutsch
Followers: 6,364
The Big Idea with Donny Deutsch

Celebrity Tweets
Just dropped my youngest off at her first day of school... More difficult than I thought it would be.
@Donny_Deutsch (Donny Deutsch)

Simon Cowell
@SimonPCowell
Followers: 7,095
American Idol

Janice Dickinson
@JDintheJungle
Followers: 15,922
The Janice Dickinson Modeling Agency

Celebrity Tweets
But it also really scared me, I really hope and pray to God that nothing like that ever happens. What are your thoughts on this 2012 theory?
@ParisHilton (Paris Hilton)

Cindy Crawford
@CindyCrawford
Followers: 205,652
Supermodel, spokesperson

Annie Duke
@RealAnnieDuke
Followers: 16,901
Professional poker player

Celebrity Tweets
Ha some of these messages really do make me laugh, and some make me feeeeel ......
slightly sick
@SimonPCowell (Simon Cowell)

Personalities

John C. Dvorak
@THErealDVORAK
Followers: 63,214
Vice-President of Mevio

Chelsea Handler
@chelsealately
Followers: 1,777,389
The Chelsea Lately Show

Celebrity Tweets
just talked to @ladygaga. Her mgmt didnt want her to do 2nd album (the fame monster) but she secretly wrote it behind their backs.
@RyanSeacrest (Ryan Seacrest)

Damien Fahey
@damienFahey
Followers: 10,054
I'm a Celebrity…Get Me Out of Here! host

Bob Harper
@MyTrainerBob
Followers: 31,756
The Biggest Loser fitness expert

Kevin Frazier
@KevinFrazierET
Followers: 3,473
Entertainment Tonight

Elisabeth Hasselbeck
@ehasselbeck
Followers: 138,631
The View

Celebrity Tweets
Go ahead slobber all over New Moon. But for the soul see The Messenger or An Education or Precious or anything with a heart and mind.
@petertravers (Peter Travers)

Mark Geragos
@markgeragos
Followers: 3,160
Attorney

Courtney Hazlett
@courtneyatmsnbc
Followers: 2,825
Celebrity correspondent, msnbc.com

Jon Gosselin
@jongosselin1
Followers: 75,305
Jon & Kate Plus 8

Hugh Hefner
@hughhefner
Followers: 159,584
Playboy Enterprises

Celebrity Tweets
I find it funny that it's on Digg that I'm here. I'm looking forward to when people can have unlimited connections on Facebook soon!
@finkd (Mark Zuckerberg)

The Celebrity Tweet Directory

Celebrity Tweets
"A lot of people have imagination, but can't execute--you have to execute with the imagination." --Donald J. Trump
@realDonaldTrump (Donald J. Trump)

Joanna Hernandez
@cocktailvh1
Followers: 41,901
For the Love of Ray J

Paris Hilton
@ParisHilton
Followers: 1,031,979
Paris Hilton's My New BFF

Perez Hilton
@PerezHilton
Followers: 1,623,204
Perezhilton.com

Derek Hough
@OfficialDHough
Followers: 34,038
Dancing with the Stars

Kathy Ireland
@kathyireland
Followers: 27,518
Kathy Ireland Worldwide

Jesse James
@Frankyluckman
Followers: 8,706
West Coast Choppers

Celebrity Tweets
A tip to my readers: Don't ever let Lindsay Lohan borrow anything from you.
@chelsealately (Chelsea Handler)

John Hodgman
@hodgman
Followers: 235,441
PC in Apple's "Get a Mac" campaign

Brooke Hogan
@BrookeHogan
Followers: 212,724
Hogan Knows Best, Brooke Knows Best

Kris Jenner
@KeepinUpWKris
Followers: 168,336
Keeping Up with the Kardashians

Levi Johnston
@LeviJohnston05
Followers: 4,275
Upcoming Playgirl magazine model

Celebrity Tweets
I woke up & thanked God for removing the toxicity in my life so I could "glow"...b/c now there is nothing poisoning me from the inside!
@StarJonesEsq (Star Jones)

Personalities

Star Jones
@StarJonesEsq
Followers: 37,018
Attorney, The View

Gayle King
@kinggayle
Followers: 104,278
The Gayle King Show

Khloe Kardashian
@KhloeKardashian
Followers: 125,559
Keeping Up with the Kardashians

Larry King
@kingsthings
Followers: 1,480,562
Larry King Live

Kim Kardashian
@KimKardashian
Followers: 2,623,225
Keeping Up with the Kardashians

Karl Lagerfeld
@Karl_Lagerfeld
Followers: 147,694
Fashion designer

Celebrity Tweets
" I am who I am, I am what I am, I do what I do and I ain't never gonna do it any differ-
ent. "Buck Owens
@Fankyluckman (Jesse James)

Kourtney Kardashian
@KourtneyKardash
Followers: 663,221
Keeping Up with the Kardashians

Ricki Lake
@Msrickilake
Followers: 19,977
The Ricki Lake Show, Hair

Celebrity Tweets
Re:water on the moon-a conf of what we have long suspected-but it doesn't suggest a
commercial Gold Rush or make that Water Rush-to the moon
@therealBuzz (Buzz Aldrin)

Emma Kennedy
@EmmaK67
Followers: 8,176
Actress, writer

Padma Lakshmi
@PadmaLakshmi
Followers: 13,550
Top Chef

Celebrity Tweets
@ Reggie_Bush Wait and see what I put in your stocking this year ;-)
@KimKardashian (Kim Kardashian)

The Celebrity Tweet Directory

Shayne Lamas
@ShayneDahlLamas
Followers: 8,659
The Bachelor, Leave it to Lamas

Dina Lohan
@dinalohan
Followers: 6,139
Living Lohan

Amanda Leatherman
@MandaLeatherman
Followers: 2,285
FSN, PokerRoad.com

Holly Madison
@hollymadison123
Followers: 250,050
The Girls Next Door

Adam Leber
@AdamLeber
Followers: 10,114
Manager, Britney Spears

Howie Mandel
@howiemmandel
Followers: 13,123
Deal or No Deal

Celebrity Tweets
Thurs Challenge, Cut your calories by 200 today AND burn 200 more calories in your workout. Creating that deficit helps with weight loss.
@MyTrainerBob (Bob Harper)

Harvey Levin
@HarveyLevinTMZ
Followers: 109,035
TMZ executive producer

Erin Manning
@ErinManning
Followers: 242
The Whole Picture

Celebrity Tweets
just got home, let out the dogs, within minutes they cornered, attacked and killed an opossum. had to wash little bloody mouths .life on farm
@MarthaStewart (Martha Stewart)

Mark Lisanti
@marklisanti
Followers: 3,435
Gossip monger, blogger

Bridget Marquardt
@BunnyBridget
Followers: 172,687
The Girls Next Door

Ali Lohan
@alilohan
Followers: 11,151
Living Lohan

Mike Massimino
@Astro_Mike
Followers: 1,176,169
Astronaut

Personalities

Stella McCartney
@StellaMcCartney
Followers: 27,645
Fashion designer

David Mitchell
@RealDMitchell
Followers: 120,226
Peep Show

Celebrity Tweets
We should always take our 1st impression. If we meet someone & a small alarm goes off-run! Darkness pulls us down. Light lifts us up to God
@Sylvia_Browne (Sylvia Browne)

Dr. Phil McGraw
@DrPhil
Followers: 231,341
Author, psychologist

Heidi Montag
@heidimontag
Followers: 816,978
The Hills

Jason Mesnick
@jason_mesnick
Followers: 13,882
The Bachelor

Walt Mossberg
@waltmossberg
Followers: 28,635
The Wall Street Journal

Jillian Michaels
@JillianMichaels
Followers: 66,138
The Biggest Loser fitness expert

Jayde Nicole
@Jayde_Nicole
Followers: 94,057
2008 Playboy Playmate of the Year

Celebrity Tweets
1/3 of the world's open water sharks face extinction, new study on White Shark Cafe will help in their protection
@JMCousteau (Jean-Michel Cousteau)

Mia Michaels
@mmraw
Followers: 18,900
So You Think You Can Dance?

Nancy O'Dell
@NancyODell
Followers: 26,035
Access Hollywood

Cesar Millan
@cesarmillan
Followers: 66,287
The Dog Whisperer

Yoko Ono
@yokoono
Followers: 567,337
Artist, musician

Jack Osbourne
@MrJackO
Followers: 40,815
The Osbournes

Andi Peters
@xxandip
Followers: 76,416
Presenter, voice actor, executive

Kelly Osbourne
@MissKellyO
Followers: 191,366
The Osbournes, Dancing with the Stars

Dr. Drew Pinsky
@drdrew
Followers: 1,686,429
The Man Show, Celebrity Rehab

Celebrity Tweets
"All human life must be protected, especially that of the weak and suffering..."
@Pope_Benedict (Pope benedict)

Sharon Osbourne
@MrsSOsbourne
Followers: 111,148
The Osbournes, The X Factor

Mark Polansky
@Astro_127
Followers: 40,516
Astronaut

Dr. Mehmet Oz
@DrOz
Followers: 83,643
Cardiothoracic surgeon, The Dr. OZ Show

Whitney Port
@whitneyEVEport
Followers: 324,743
The Hills

Petros Papadakis
@PetrosAndMoney
Followers: 6,477
Fox Sports Radio

Spencer Pratt
@spencerpratt
Followers: 630,247
The Hills

Audrina Patridge
@OfficialAudrina
Followers: 440,961
The Hills

Stephanie Pratt
@stephaniepratt
Followers: 266,362
The Hills

Celebrity Tweets
Disease, Natural disasters, fate do not discriminate, but terrorism does. It discriminates against the innocent.
@QueenRania (Rania Al Abdullah)

Personalities

Katie Price
@**MissKatiePrice**
Followers: 445,082
Author, model

Jonathan Ross
@**Wossy**
Followers: 452,457
Film critic, radio/TV presenter

Giuliana Rancic
@**GiulianaRancic**
Followers: 1,494,400
E! News

Phillip Schofield
@**Schofe**
Followers: 275,132
TV presenter

Doug Reinhardt
@**DougReinhardt1**
Followers: 19,457
The Hills

Robert Scoble
@**Scobleizer**
Followers: 104,554
Scobleizer

Nicole Richie
@**nicolerichie**
Followers: 749,431
The Simple Life

Ryan Seacrest
@**RyanSeacrest**
Followers: 2,623,938
TV producer, American Idol, E! News

Joan Rivers
@**Joan_Rivers**
Followers: 57,078
Comedian, TV host

Courtenay Semel
@**Courtenaysemel**
Followers: 5,031
Filthy Rich: Cattle Drive

Celebrity Tweets
What are we doing? Changing the question to "What's happening?" Carry on with your normal tweeting.
@**ev (Evan Williams)**

Melissa Rivers
@**MelRivers**
Followers: 7,013
TV host

Terri Seymour
@**TerriSeymour**
Followers: 1,362
The X Factor

Shaun Robinson
@**shaunssanctuary**
Followers: 4,507
Access Hollywood

Adam Shankman
@**adammshankman**
Followers: 48,047
Choreographer

Celebrity Tweets
Britney's body is back. Pre-meltdown days!
@HarveyLevinTMZ (Harvey Levin)

Sherri Sheperd
@SherriESheperd
Followers: 156,866
The View

Stephen A Smith
@stephenasmith
Followers: 42,761
Quite Frankly with Stephen A. Smith

Richard Simmons
@TheWeightSaint
Followers: 3,061
Fitness guru

Lara Spencer
@TILaraSpencer
Followers: 4,229
The Insider

Kimora Lee Simmons
@BabyPhat
Followers: 79,546
Phat, Baby Phat

Mark Steines
@MarkSteinesET
Followers: 2,688
Entertainment Tonight

Tavis Smiley
@tavissmiley
Followers: 51,211
Tavis Smiley, The Tavis Smiley Show

Martha Stewart
@MarthaStewart
Followers: 1,696,891
Martha Stewart Living Omnimedia

Karina Smirnoff
@Karina_Smirnoff
Followers: 9,852
Dancing with the Stars

Ryan Sutter
@ryansutter
Followers: 3,779
The Bachelorette

Kenny Smith
@TheJetOnTNT
Followers: 53,491
Inside the NBA

Trista Sutter
@tristasutter
Followers: 13,071
The Bachelorette

Celebrity Tweets
unbelievable, 3 days after @drdrew suffers the loss of his Dad he saves the life of a 15 year old on the football field last night.
@markgeragos (Mark Geragos)

Personalities

John Tesh
@JohnTesh
Followers: 4,691
John Tesh Radio Show

Tila Tequila
@OfficialTila
Followers: 266,354
A Shot at Love with Tila Tequila

Peter Travers
@petertravers
Followers: 8,158
Rolling Stone movie critic

Donald J. Trump
@realDonaldTrump
Followers: 18,771
Trump Organization, Chairman/CEO

Ivanka Trump
@IvankaTrump
Followers: 506,198
Daughter of Ivana/Donald J. Trump

Shannon Tweed
@shannonleetweed
Followers: 13,474
Gene Simmons Family Jewels

Bob Vila
@BobVilacom
Followers: 1,094,183
This Old House

Kat Von D
@thekatvond
Followers: 112,559
Tattoo artist, L.A. Ink

Dita Von Teese
@DitaVonTeese
Followers: 186,854
Burlesque star

Jhonen Vasquez
@JhonenV
Followers: 17,156
Johnny the Homicidal Maniac

Chris Webber
@NBATVChris
Followers: 32,225
NBA TV

Kendra Wilkinson
@KendraWilkinson
Followers: 417,022
The Girls Next Door, Kendra

Evan Williams
@ev
Followers: 1,172,839
Twitter CEO

Oprah Winfrey
Oprah
Followers: 2,662,424
The Oprah Winfrey Show

Celebrity Tweets

I was on E! @thatmorningshow today talking about my new lighting kit- here's the vid http://bit.ly/3m73m0
@ErinManning (Erin Manning)

Angela Yee
@angelayee
Followers: 49,708
Radio host

Alex Zane
@alex_zane
Followers: 33,128
Rude Tube

Rachel Zoe
@rzrachelzoe
Followers: 135,566
Stylist

Mark Zuckerberg
@finkd
Followers: 27,598
Facebook CEO/Co-Founder

Politics

Political Correspondents

Patrick J.Buchanan
@PatrickBuchanan
Followers: 873
Author, Columnist, MSNBC News Analyst

Jefferson Graham
@jeffersongraham
Followers: 1,596
USA TODAY

Ana Marie Cox
@anamariecox
Followers: 1,368,614
Author, editor, founder of Wonkette

David Gregory
@davidgregory
Followers: 1,401,426
Meet the Press

Craig Crawford
@craig_crawford
Followers: 3,165
MSNBC analyst/author, blogger

Savannah Guthrie
@SavannahGuthrie
Followers: 1,215
NBC News White House Correspondent

Celebrity Tweets
My son this morning asked two questions about political parties: "why are they called parties and do they have cake?"
@davidgregory (David Gregory)

Candy Crowley
@crowleyCNN
Followers: 2,624
Senior Political Reporter, CNN

Burt Helm
@BurtHelm
Followers: 1,262
BusinessWeek

John Dickerson
@jdickerson
Followers: 1,334,776
Slate correspondent, CBS News analysis

Arik Hesseldah
@ahess247
Followers: 3,866
BusinessWeek

Amy Feldman
@amyfeldman
Followers: 2,968
Business Week

John King
@JohnKingCNN
Followers: 2,255
State of the Union with John King

Politics

Anne Kornblut
@annekornblut
Followers: 2,875
The Washington Post

Dan Patterson
@DanPatterson
Followers: 6,523
ABC News

Howard Kurtz
@HowardKurtz
Followers: 15,067
Reliable Sources

Jon Ralston
@RalstonFlash
Followers: 1,020
Face to Face, Las Vegas Sun

Meghan McCain
@McCainBlogette
Followers: 77,102
Political blogger

Bob Schieffer
@bobschieffer
Followers: 6,568
Face the Nation, CBS News correspondent

Mike Murphy
@murphymike
Followers: 3,688
Republican political consultant

Rev. Al Sharpton
@TheRevAl
Followers: 16,080
Activist, Baptist Minister

NBC First Read
@NBCFirstRead
Followers: 1,268
NBC News political unit

Brian Stelter
@brianstelter
Followers: 14,744
The New York Times

Norah O'Donnell
@NorahODonnell
Followers: 9,072
MSNBC Chief Washington Correspondent

George Stephanopoulos
@GStephanopoulos
Followers: 1,512,361
ABC News Chief Washington Correspondent

Chuck Todd
@chucktodd
Followers: 9,120
NBC Chief White House Correspondent

Joe Trippi
@JoeTrippi
Followers: 1,007,185
Democratic consultant, author

Political Pundits

Glenn Beck
@glennbeck
Followers: 163,186
Conservative Fox News television host

Rush Limbaugh
@limbaugh
Followers: 52,424
The Rush Limbaugh Show

Celebrity Tweets
I just realized my tonsils are missing. Man, I wish I were as rich as M. Moore i could've had some of that sweet Castro Care he loves.
@glennbeck (Glenn Beck)

Sean Hannity
@hannityshow
Followers: 45,541
Hannity and Colmes

Celebrity Tweets
The Gratitude Wave: Showing Our Soldiers We Have NOT Forgotten Them: "Thousands of men and women have...http://bit.ly/3KRQXI
@hannityshow (Sean Hannity)

Politicians

Dick Armey
@DickArmey
Followers: 7,309
FreedomWorks Chairman

Joe Biden
@joebiden
Followers: 30,496
Vice President (D)

Politics

Mike Bloomberg
@mikebloomberg
Followers: 14,346
Mayor, New York City, NY (I)

Eric Cantor
@GOPWhip
Followers: 6,359
House, Republican Whip

John Boehner
@johnboehner
Followers: 18,760
House, Minority Leader (R)

Anh Joseph Cao
@AnhJosephCao
Followers: 2,053
Congressman, Louisiana (R)

John Boozman
@JohnBoozman
Followers: 2,971
Congressman, Arkansas (R)

Wes Clark
@GeneralClark
Followers: 826
Retired US 4-star General

Barbara Boxer
@Barbara_Boxer
Followers: 17,232
Senator, California (D)

Susan Collins
@senatorcollins
Followers: 4,705
Senator, Maine (R)

Jerry Brown
@JerryBrown2010
Followers: 1,020,255
Attorney General, California (D)

Charlie Crist
@charliecristfl
Followers: 3,568
Governor, Florida (R)

Michael Burgess, MD
@michaelcburgess
Followers: 3,785
Congressman, Texas (R)

John Culberson
@johnculberson
Followers: 13,045
Congressman, Texas (R)

The Celebrity Tweet Directory

Howard Dean
@deanforamerica
Followers: 55
Democratic National Committee

Tom DeLay
@tomdelay
Followers: 3,330
Former Representative, Texas (R)

Jim DeMint
@JimDeMint
Followers: 28,488
Senator, South Carolina (R)

Chris Dodd
@SenChrisDodd
Followers: 10,060
Senator, Connecticut (D)

John Edwards
@johnedwards
Followers: 14,688
Former Senator, North Carolina (D)

Keith Ellison
@keithellison
Followers: 4,776
Congressman, Minnesota (D)

John Ensign
@JohnEnsign
Followers: 6,256
Senator, Nevada (R)

Carly Fiorina
@CarlyforCA
Followers: 71,801
Senate candidate, California (R)

Randy Forbes
@Randy_Forbes
Followers: 2,096
Representative, Virginia (R)

Al Franken
@alfranken
Followers: 2,057
Junior Senator, Minnesota (D)

Newt Gingrich
@newtgingrich
Followers: 1,197,536
Former House Speaker (R), FOX News analyst

Al Gore
@algore
Followers: 1,909,967
Former Vice President (D)

Lindsey Graham
@GrahamBlog
Followers: 1,361
Senator, South Carolina (R)

Chuck Grassley
@ChuckGrassley
Followers: 17,486
Senator, Iowa (R)

Celebrity Tweets
Michigan-thx 4 Going Rogue! Perfect tour kickoff w/Kid Rock tune praising Northern MI humming in backgrnd @ Barnes/Noble. Above expectations
@SarahPalinUSA (Sarah Palin)

Politics

Alan Grayson
@AlanGrayson
Followers: 3,835
Representative, Florida (D)

John Kerry
@JohnKerry
Followers: 3,685
Senator, Massachusetts (D)

Pete Hoekstra
@petehoekstra
Followers: 8,790
Congressman, Michigan (R)

Bob Latta
@boblatta
Followers: 4,622
Congressman, Ohio (R)

Jim Inhofe
@jiminhofe
Followers: 4,986
Senator, Oklahoma (R)

Kevin Madden
@KevinMaddenDC
Followers: 3,119
Republican strategist

Jesse Jackson Jr.
@JacksonJrOnline
Followers: 1,963
Congressman, Illinois (D)

John McCain
@SenJohnMcCain
Followers: 1,592,342
Senator, Arizona (R)

Bobby Jindal
@BobbyJindal
Followers: 36,610
Governor, Louisiana (R)

Claire McCaskill
@clairecmc
Followers: 34,857
Senator, Missouri (D)

Boris Johnson
@MayorOfLondon
Followers: 57,117
Mayor of London, England

George Miller
@askgeorge
Followers: 2,341
Congressman, California (D)

Jim Moran
@Jim_Moran
Followers: 744
Congressman, Virginia (D)

Karl Rove
@KarlRove
Followers: 93,178
Sr. Advisor, President George W. Bush

Admiral Mike Mullen
@thejointstaff
Followers: 8,927
Chairman, Joint Chiefs of Staff

Tim Ryan
@timryan
Followers: 3,644
Congressman, Ohio (D)

Gavin Newsom
@GavinNewsom
Followers: 1,259,161
Mayor, San Francisco, CA (D)

Rick Santorum
@senrick58
Followers: 723
Former Senator, Pennsylvania (R)

Barack Obama
@BarackObama
Followers: 2,716,743
44th President (D)

Dave Schultheis
@Sen_Schultheis
Followers: 382
State Senator, Colorado Springs, CO (R)

Sarah Palin
@SarahPalinUSA
Followers: 25,847
Former Governor, Alaska (R)

Chuck Schumer
@ChuckSchumer
Followers: 2,074
Senator, New York (D)

Celebrity Tweets
Check out Google Earth Climate Tour
@algore (Al Gore)

Harry Reid
@SenatorReid
Followers: 4,363
Senator, Nevada (D)

Arnold Schwarzenegger
@Schwarzenegger
Followers: 1,428,649
Governor, California (R)

Celebrity Tweets
Having coffee with a few CT residents visiting DC. I do this a few times a month so
check my website if you are planning a trip down.
@SenChrisDodd (Chris Dodd)

Politics

Joe Sestak
@JoeSestak
Followers: 2,533
Congressman, Pennsylvania (D)

Antonio Villaraigosa
@villaraigosa
Followers: 12,912
Mayor, Los Angeles, CA (D)

Arlen Specter
@SenArlenSpecter
Followers: 6,719
Senator, Pennsylvania (D)

David Vitter
@DavidVitter
Followers: 3,120
Junior Senator, Louisiana (R)

 Celebrity Tweets
About to enjoy Texas BBQ with LSU Coach Mainieri, care of Governor Rick Perry. Congratulations Tigers!
@BobbyJindal (Bobby Jindal)

Fred Thompson
@fredthompson
Followers: 24,026
Former Senator, Tennessee (R)

Joe Wilson
@CongJoeWilson
Followers: 13,354
Congressman, South Carolina (R)

Maxime Verhagen
@MaximeVerhagen
Followers: 23,686
Foreign Affairs Minister, Netherlands

Rob Wittman
@RobWittman
Followers: 2,943
Representative, Virginia (R)

Celebrity Tweets
Lindsey Graham: "What awaits us when we bring a 9/11 conspirator like KSM into federal court? Chaos. His trial will be a zoo."
@GrahamBlog (Lindsey Graham)

Sports

Baseball (MLB)

Jeremy Affeldt
@JeremyAffeldt
Followers: 1,628
San Francisco Giants, Pitcher

Billy Butler
@BillyButlerKC
Followers: 406
Kansas City Royals, 1st Baseman

Celebrity Tweets
on the way to the field doesn't get better then Red Sox-Yankees
@davidortiz (David Ortiz)

Rod Allen
@RodAllen12
Followers: 2,114
Retired, Detroit Tigers, Outfielder

Jose Canseco
@JoseCanseco
Followers: 146,798
Retired, Montreal Expos, Outfielder

Jeremy Barfield
@jeremybarfield
Followers: 181
Oakland Athletics, 2nd Baseman

Joe Carter
@JoeCarter_29
Followers: 1,558
Retired, San Francisco Giants, Right Fielder

Celebrity Tweets
Players should be smart enough to realize the Steroid era is over and the game should be clean. The risk/reward isn't worth it today!
@JoseCanseco (Jose Canseco)

Carlos Beltran
@carlosbeltran15
Followers: 943
New York Mets, Outfielder

Roger Clemens
@rogerclemens
Followers: 1,607
Retired, Yankees, Pitcher

Craig Breslow
@CraigBreslow
Followers: 299
Oakland Athletics, Pitcher

Covelli Crisp
@Coco_Crisp
Followers: 7,452
Kansas City Royals, Outfielder

Sports

Carlos Delgado
@carlosdelgado21
Followers: 7,102
New York Mets, 1st Baseman

Matt Kemp
@mattkemp27
Followers: 9,893
Los Angeles Dodgers, Outfielder

Chad Durbin
@ShowcaseU
Followers: 5,189
Philadelphia Phillies, Pitcher

Tony La Russa
@TonyLaRussa
Followers: 3,036
St. Louis Cardinals, Manager

Jason Grilli
@GrillCheese49
Followers: 5,475
Texas Rangers, Pitcher

Matt LaPorta
@Gator4God
Followers: 2,969
Cleveland Indians, Outfielder

Blake Hawksworth
@BlakeHawksworth
Followers: 1,485
St. Louis Cardinals, Pitcher

Tommy Lasorda
@TommyLasorda
Followers: 5,003
Retired, LA Dodgers, Manager

Dirk Hayhurst
@TheGarfoose
Followers: 384
Toronto Blue Jays, Pitcher

Francisco Liriano
@liriano47
Followers: 178
Minnesota Twins, Pitcher

Orlando Hudson
@orlandohudson
Followers: 4,350
Los Angeles Dodgers, 2nd Baseman

Steve Lyons
@STEVELYONS2
Followers: 750
Retired, Boston Red Sox, Outfielder

The Celebrity Tweet Directory

Joe Maddon
@RaysJoeMaddon
Followers: 6,043
Tampa Bay Devil Rays, Manager

David Ortiz
@davidortiz
Followers: 15,917
Boston Red Sox, Designated Hitter

Celebrity Tweets
Men of genius are admired. Men of wealth are envied. Men of power are feared, but only men of character are trusted. - Arthur Friedman
@JeremyAffeldt (Jeremy Affeldt)

Reid Mahon
@DBackPlates22
Followers: 104
Arizona Diamondbacks, Pitcher

Matt Pagnozzi
@MattPagnozzi
Followers: 342
St. Louis Cardinals, Catcher

Seth McClung
@73_MC
Followers: 961
Milwaukee Brewers, Pitcher

Jarrod Parker
@JarrodBParker
Followers: 51
Arizona Diamondbacks, Pitcher

Justin Morneau
@JustinMorneau
Followers: 8,504
Minnesota Twins, 1st Baseman

Jorge Posada
@newjorgeposada
Followers: 4,959
New York Yankees, Catcher

Jamie Moyer
@moyerfoundation
Followers: 1,897
Retired, Philadelphia Phillies, Pitcher

Cal Ripken Jr.
@MLBonTBSCal
Followers: 1,333
Retired, Baltimore Orioles, Shortstop

Joe Nathan
@JoeNathan36
Followers: 3,297
Minnesota Twins, Pitcher

Ryan Rowland-Smith
@hyphen18
Followers: 3,195
Seattle Mariners, Pitcher

Celebrity Tweets
Man! This is so crazy and hella fun! I love New York!
@NickSwisher (Nick Swisher)

CC Sabathia
@CC_Sabathia
Followers: 35,691
New York Yankees, Pitcher

Rich Thompson
@chopper63
Followers: 1,077
Los Angeles Angels, Pitcher

Curt Schilling
@gehrig38
Followers: 14,697
Retired, Boston Red Sox, Pitcher

Chien Ming Wang
@ChienMingWang
Followers: 986
New York Yankees, Pitcher

Joakim Soria
@joakimsoria
Followers: 2,567
Kansas City Royals, Pitcher

Todd Wellemeyer
@Todalion
Followers: 2,821
St. Louis Cardinals, Pitcher

Nick Swisher
@NickSwisher
Followers: 1,047,260
New York Yankees, 1st Baseman/Outfielder

C.J. Wilson
@str8edgeracer
Followers: 11,508
Texas Rangers, Pitcher

Mark Teahen
@ESPY_TEAHEN
Followers: 2,114
Kansas City Royals, Infielder

Basketball (NBA)

Kareem Abdul-Jabbar
@kaj33
Followers: 1,014,289
Retired, Los Angeles Lakers, Center

Chris Andersen
@Birdmancamp
Followers: 1,507
Denver Nuggets, Center/Forward

Joe Alexander
@SeeJoeDunk
Followers: 1,516
Milwaukee Bucks, Forward

Carmelo Anthony
@carmeloanthony
Followers: 35,502
Denver Nuggets, Forward

The Celebrity Tweet Directory

Trevor Ariza
@TA_Iam1
Followers: 2,522
Houston Rockets, Forward

Chris Bosh
@chrisbosh
Followers: 77,767
Toronto Raptors, Forward

Celebrity Tweets
Your prayers & good wishes really lift my spirit & helps me understand that I did the right thing by sharing this. Bless you one & all!
@Kaj33 (Kareem Abdul-Jabbar)

Ron Artest
@96TruwarierQB
Followers: 37,097
Los Angeles Lakers, Forward/Guard

Jon Brockman
@MrJonBrockman
Followers: 147,762
Sacramento Kings, Forward

Jerryd Bayless
@JBay4
Followers: 7,856
Portland Trail Blazers, Guard

Aaron Brooks
@Thirty2zero
Followers: 6,851
Houston Rockets, Guard

Celebrity Tweets
What will I miss about the game when I'm done? The game itself. Not the perks, locker room. I will miss the show. There is no better game.
@mikejames7 (Mike James)

Charlie Bell
@flintstone14
Followers: 5,264
Milwaukee Bucks, Guard

Bobby Brown
@BBROWNsix
Followers: 1,161
New Orleans Hornets, Guard

DeJuan Blair
@DeJuan45
Followers: 6,861
San Antonio Spurs, Forward

Rasual Butler
@RasualButler45
Followers: 8,814
Los Angeles Clippers, Forward

Andrew Bogut
@AndrewMBogut
Followers: 12,552
Milwaukee Bucks, Center

Brian Cardinal
@Cardinal_Brian
Followers: 3,016
Minnesota Timberwolves, Forward

Mario Chalmers
@mister6clutch
Followers: 153,252
Miami Heat, Guard

Mark Cuban
@mcuban
Followers: 111,292
Dallas Mavericks, Owner

Tyson Chandler
@tysonchandler
Followers: 22,348
Charlotte Bobcats, Center

Stephen Curry
@StephenCurry30
Followers: 31,735
Golden State Warriors, Guard

Speedy Claxton
@speeddeamon
Followers: 3,505
Atlanta Hawks, Guard

Baron Davis
@Baron_Davis
Followers: 84,282
Los Angeles Clippers, Guard

Nick Collison
@nickcollison4
Followers: 7,543
Oklahoma City Thunder, Forward

Austin Daye
@Adaye5
Followers: 3,490
Detroit Pistons, Forward

Mike Conley
@mconley11
Followers: 2,435
Memphis Grizzlies, Guard

Chris Douglas-Roberts
@cdouglasroberts
Followers: 7,500
New Jersey Nets, Guard

Celebrity Tweets
In baseball isn't strange that they are playing a sport while wearing belts and some-
times turtlenecks & coaches wear uniforms?
@Mconley11 (Mike Conley)

Daequan Cook
@3ptChamp
Followers: 5,981
Miami Heat, Guard

Jared Dudley
@JaredDudley619
Followers: 8,671
Phoenix Suns, Forward

Joe Crawford
@JoeCrawford5
Followers: 6,166
New York Nicks, Guard

Kevin Durant
@KevinDurant35
Followers: 84,391
Oklahoma City Thunder, Forward

The Celebrity Tweet Directory

Celebrity Tweets
Woman on train next to me has chewed thru 2 packs of nicorette gum and we r not out of Connecticut yet.
@troy_murphy (Troy Murphy)

Reggie Evans
@ReggieEvans30
Followers: 2,179
Toronto Raptors, Forward

TJ Ford
@tj_ford
Followers: 12,752
Indiana Pacers, Guard

Tyreke Evans
@thetyrekeevans
Followers: 6,497
Sacramento Kings, Guard

Rick Fox
@Rickafox
Followers: 25,769
Retired, Los Angeles Lakers, Forward

Rudy Fernandez
@rudy5fernandez
Followers: 34,387
Portland Trail Blazers, Guard

Randy Foye
@randyfoye
Followers: 9,250
Washington Wizards, Guard

Michael Finley
@Da_Finster
Followers: 3,791
San Antonio Spurs, Forward/Guard

Adonal Foyle
@afoyle3131
Followers: 1,695
Orlando Magic, Center

Celebrity Tweets
Funny quote I heard after the wiz game "Charlie it seem like u ran out of bullets, towards the end of the game, so u threw the gun at him"
@CV31 (Charlie Villanueva)

Derek Fisher
@derekfisher
Followers: 238,315
Los Angeles Lakers, Guard

Francisco Garcia
@cisco32
Followers: 150,584
Sacramento Kings, Forward/Guard

Jonny Flynn
@J_Flynn
Followers: 7,676
Minnesota Timberwolves, Guard

Rudy Gay
@rudygay22
Followers: 34,984
Memphis Grizzlies, Forward

Manu Ginobili
@manuginobili
Followers: 39,832
San Antonio Spurs, Guard

Tyler Hansbrough
@THANS50
Followers: 6,977
Indiana Pacers, Forward

Ryan Gomes
@GotGomes
Followers: 1,891
Minnesota Timberwolves, Forward

James Harden
@jHARD13
Followers: 8,822
Oklahoma City Thunder, Guard

Drew Gooden
@DrewGooden
Followers: 8,762
Dallas Mavericks, Center/Forward

Al Harrington
@a7harrington
Followers: 2,537
New York Nicks, Forward

Celebrity Tweets
Thought of the day: Most people die coming down from Mt. Everest not going up!
@Da_Finster (Michael Finley)

Danny Granger
@dgranger33
Followers: 18,472
Indiana Pacers, Forward/Guard

Devin Harris
@devin34harris
Followers: 4,801
New Jersey Nets, Guard

Jeff Green
@jeff_green22
Followers: 6,125
Oklahoma City Thunder, Forward

Luther Head
@Luther_Head
Followers: 439
Indiana Pacers, Guard

Donté Greene
@DonteGreene
Followers: 8,435
Sacramento Kings, Forward

George Hill
@George_Hill3
Followers: 1,651
San Antonio Spurs, Guard

Blake Griffin
@blakegriffin
Followers: 45,468
Los Angeles Clippers, Forward

Al Horford
@Al_Horford
Followers: 3,543
Atlanta Hawks, Forward

Dwight Howard
@**DwightHoward**
Followers: 1,280,421
Orlando Magic, Center

DeAndre Jordan
@**deandrejordan**
Followers: 7,254
Los Angeles Clippers, Center

Josh Howard
@**joshhoward5**
Followers: 7,516
Dallas Mavericks, Forward

Carl Landry
@**carllandry14**
Followers: 1,062
Houston Rockets, Forward

Celebrity Tweets
When all is said and done... Don't let more be said than done.
@**quietstorm_32 (CJ Watson)**

Kris Humphries
@**KrisHumphries**
Followers: 921
Dallas Mavericks, Forward

Rashard Lewis
@**Rashard_Lewis**
Followers: 22,101
Orlando Magic, Forward

Andre Iguodala
@**AI9**
Followers: 26,858
Philadelphia 76ers, Forward/Guard

Robin Lopez
@**eegabeeva88**
Followers: 2,209
Phoenix Suns, Center

Allen Iverson
@**alleniverson**
Followers: 76,572
Free Agent, Guard

Kevin Love
@**kevin_love**
Followers: 39,833
Minnesota Timberwolves, Center/Forward

Jarrett Jack
@**Jarrettjack03**
Followers: 3,267
Toronto Raptors, Guard

Kyle Lowry
@**Klow7**
Followers: 3,061
Houston Rockets, Guard

Mike James
@**mikejames7**
Followers: 2,905
Washington Wizards, Guard

Mark Madsen
@**madsen_mark**
Followers: 7,611
Retired, Minnesota Timberwolves, Forward

Sports

Shawn Marion
@matrix31
Followers: 36,106
Dallas Mavericks, Forward

Roger Mason Jr.
@MoneyMase
Followers: 9,575
San Antonio Spurs, Guard

Mike Miller
@m33m
Followers: 7,489
Minnesota Timberwolves, Guard

Patrick Mills
@Patty_Mills
Followers: 4,556
Portland Trail Blazers, Guard

Celebrity Tweets
Everyone gets dunked on. Everyone. Lebron, release the tape, and don't be a cry baby.
@dennisrodman (Dennis Rodman)

Sean May
@BigMay42
Followers: 5,466
Sacramento Kings, Forward

Eric Maynor
@EMaynor3
Followers: 4,255
Utah Jazz, Guard

JaVale McGee
@bigdaddywookie
Followers: 2,052
Washington Wizards, Center

Jodie Meeks
@JMEEKS23
Followers: 11,724
Milwaukee Bucks, Guard

C.J. Miles
@CJMiles34
Followers: 4,171
Utah Jazz, Forward/Guard

Yao Ming
@YaoMing
Followers: 7,092
Houston Rockets, Center

Nazr Mohammed
@NazrMohammed
Followers: 5,228
Charlotte Bobcats, Center/Forward

Anthony Morrow
@BlackBoiPachino
Followers: 2,334
Golden State Warriors, Guard

Troy Murphy
@troy_murphy
Followers: 6,237
Indiana Pacers, Forward

Steve Nash
@the_real_nash
Followers: 100,247
Phoenix Suns, Guard

The Celebrity Tweet Directory

Celebrity Tweets
Most fun part of owning team. Charging court after buzzer beat...knowing the cops aren't behind you)
@mcuban (Mark Cuban)

Fabricio Oberto
@obricio7
Followers: 150,661
Washington Wizards, Center/Forward

Tony Parker
@tp9network
Followers: 2,425
San Antonio Spurs, Guard

Patrick O'Bryant
@13POB13
Followers: 2,724
Toronto Raptors, Center

Chris Paul
@Oneandonlycp3
Followers: 69,308
New Orleans Hornets, Guard

Lamar Odom
@RealLamarOdom
Followers: 316,640
Los Angeles Lakers, Forward/Guard

Morris Peterson
@mopete24
Followers: 5,193
New Orleans Hornets, Forward/Guard

Jermaine O'Neal
@jermaineoneal
Followers: 14,751
Miami Heat, Center/Forward

Johan Petro
@Frenchi27
Followers: 146,944
Denver Nuggets, Center

Shaquille O'Neil
@THE_REAL_SHAQ
Followers: 2,545,155
Cleveland Cavaliers, Center

Paul Pierce
@paulpierce34
Followers: 1,320,410
Boston Celtics, Forward

Travis Outlaw
@Travis25Outlaw
Followers: 5,787
Portland Trail Blazers, Forward

Jason Richardson
@jrich23
Followers: 28,264
Phoenix Suns, Forward/Guard

Zaza Pachulia
@zaza27
Followers: 4,152
Atlanta Hawks, Center/Forward

Quentin Richardson
@QRich
Followers: 228,908
Miami Heat, Forward/Guard

Nate Robinson
@nate_robinson
Followers: 38,823
New York Nicks, Guard

Dennis Rodman
@dennisrodman
Followers: 10,629
Retired, Dallas Mavericks, Forward

Ricky Rubio
@rickyrubio9
Followers: 35,577
FC Barcelona, Guard

Bryon Russell
@BRuss3
Followers: 1,495
Retired, Utah Jazz, Guard

Detlef Schrempf
@Dschrempf
Followers: 16,932
Retired, Portland Trail Blazers, Forward

Thabo Sefolosha
@ThaboSefolosha
Followers: 3,720
Oklahoma City Thunder, Guard

Craig Smith
@Csmeezy5
Followers: 922
Los Angeles Clippers, Forward

Amar'e Stoudemire
@Amareisreal
Followers: 39,005
Phoenix Suns, Forward

DaJuan Summers
@dsummers35
Followers: 5,276
Detroit Pistons, Forward

Jason Terry
@jasonterry31
Followers: 162,853
Dallas Mavericks, Guard

Hasheem Thabeet
@HasheemTheDream
Followers: 18,452
Memphis Grizzlies, Center

Jason Thompson
@jtthekid
Followers: 7,598
Sacramento Kings, Center/Forward

Charlie Villanueva
@CV31
Followers: 61,689
Detroit Pistons, Forward

Sasha Vujacic
@SashaVujacic
Followers: 32,916
Los Angeles Lakers, Guard

Celebrity Tweets
I hear Obama is in Shanghai, my hometown. Welcome to China. Hope you enjoy. Like NYC, the best food is sold on streets (I know u r busy tho)
@YaoMing (Yao Ming)

The Celebrity Tweet Directory

Dwyane Wade
@dwadeofficial
Followers: 125,423
Miami Heat, Guard

Lou Williams
@TeamLou23
Followers: 4,804
Philadelphia 76ers, Guard

CJ Watson
@quietstorm_32
Followers: 147,283
Golden State Warriors, Guard

Mo Williams
@mogotti2
Followers: 33,224
Cleveland Cavaliers, Guard

Kyle Weaver
@kyleweaver5
Followers: 1,039
Oklahoma City Thunder, Guard

Shelden Williams
@SheldenWilliams
Followers: 7,345
Boston Celtics, Center/Forward

Celebrity Tweets
Almost moved into my place in DC... Just bought a new plasma and direct tv guys r hooking me up... FAVRE a Viking, we r Super Bowl bound!!!
@m33m (Mike Miller)

Sonny Weems
@Sonny13
Followers: 2,859
Toronto Raptors, Guard

Dorell Wright
@DWRIGHTWAY
Followers: 16,930
Miami Heat, Forward

Russell Westbrook
@russwest44
Followers: 15,240
Oklahoma City Thunder, Guard

Julian Wright
@jujubee32
Followers: 4,041
New Orleans Hornets, Forward

Celebrity Tweets
@Oprah! u r truly an inspiration to so many people, you should be awarded the nobel peace prize. Love all that you do, u r my role model.
@THE_REAL_SHAQ (Shaquille O'Neil)

Deron Williams
@D_Will_8_4real
Followers: 21,692
Utah Jazz, Guard

Thad Young
@yungsmoove21
Followers: 4,254
Philadelphia 76ers, Forward

Sam Young
@**SamYoung4**
Followers: 1,190
Memphis Grizzlies, Forward

Car Racing

Marco Andretti
@**Andretti26**
Followers: 7,125
IndyCar driver

Sarah Fisher
@**SarahFisher67**
Followers: 4,562
IndyCar driver/owner

Robby Gordan
@**RobbyGordan**
Followers: 6,365
NASCAR driver

Denny Hamlin
@**dennyhamlin**
Followers: 7,830
NASCAR driver

Kasey Kahne
@**kaseykahne**
Followers: 13,121
NASCAR driver

Tony Kanaan
@**TonyKanaan**
Followers: 58,623
IndyCar driver

Bobby Labonte
@**Bobby_Labonte**
Followers: 11,122
NASCAR driver

Ryan Newman
@**RyanNewman39**
Followers: 10,023
NASCAR driver

Juan Pablo Montoya
@**jpmontoya**
Followers: 61,426
NASCAR driver

Danica Patrick
@**DanicaPatrick**
Followers: 57,125
IndyCar/NASCAR (2010) driver

Celebrity Tweets
getting ready to head to parents to get some home made spaghetti. It's tradition. my mom went into labor with me while eating it
@**dennyhamlin (Denny Hamlin)**

The Celebrity Tweet Directory

Kyle Petty
@kylepetty
Followers: 18,349
NASCAR broadcaster

Jimmy Vasser
@jimmyvasser
Followers: 2,664
Team owner

Graham Rahal
@GrahamRahal
Followers: 3,263
IndyCar driver

Kenny Wallace
@Kenny_Wallace
Followers: 16,086
NASCAR driver

Elliott Sadler
@Elliott_Sadler
Followers: 14,008
NASCAR driver

Michael Waltrip
@mw55
Followers: 19,874
Team owner

Celebrity Tweets
I dont unpack after a trip and I have been on a few so I really have to clean my room......
I feel like a kid when I say that. Haha
@DanickaPatrick (Danica Patrick)

Tomas Scheckter
@tomasscheckter
Followers: 3,053
IndyCar driver

Dan Wheldon
@danwheldon
Followers: 3,947
IndyCar driver

Alex Tagliani
@tagliani
Followers: 2,139
NASCAR driver

Cycling

Lance Armstrong
@lancearmstrong
Followers: 2,219,735
Tour de France winner

Taylor Phinney
@taylorphinney
Followers: 12,382
World Champion

Celebrity Tweets
Confirmed - the moon has water. Let's go!
@lancearmstrong (Lance Armstrong)

Extreme Sports

Gretchen Bleiler
@GretchenBleiler
Followers: 1,996
Professional snowboarder

Rob Dyrdek
@robdyrdek
Followers: 353,328
Professional skateboarder

Bob Burnquist
@bobburnquist
Followers: 17,418
Professional skateboarder

Carey Hart
@hartluck
Followers: 84,149
Freestyle Motocross motorcycle racer

Celebrity Tweets
crashed a wedding last week at timberline lodge! slow danced with the bride, ate cake, and almost caught the bouquet!
@Shaun_White (Shaun White)

Jesse Csincsak
@Jsinsak
Followers: 2,311
Professional snowboarder

Tony Hawk
@tonyhawk
Followers: 1,841,699
Professional skateboarder

Tara Dakides
@TaraDakides
Followers: 1,691
Professional snowboarder

Bam Margera
@BAM__MARGERA
Followers: 93,049
Professional skateboarder

Celebrity Tweets
I'll be good in about 4 months that's when they take the screws out of my foot
@RyanSheckler (Ryan Sheckler)

Dave Mirra
@davemirra
Followers: 8,223
American BMX rider

Ryan Sheckler
@RyanSheckler
Followers: 1,245,377
Professional skateboarder

Celebrity Tweets
I think I'm officially a vampire. Haven't seen the sun other than going to bed in 3 days! gonna kick @pink 's ass in darts, pool, and beer!
@hartluck (Carey Hart)

Leanne Pelosi
@leannepelosi
Followers: 1,017
Professional snowboarder

Louie Vito
@louievito
Followers: 10,805
Professional snowboarder

Celebrity Tweets
Chicago: Millenium Park, there is a bridge that looks like a snake. Go to the head of it.
@tonyhawk (Tony Hawk)

Figure Skating

Jeremy Abbott
@jeremyabbottpcf
Followers: 1,243
US

Patrick Chan
@PChiddy
Followers: 2,056
Canada

Ben Agosto
@Ben_Agosto
Followers: 1,471
US

Meryl Davis
@Meryl_Davis
Followers: 574
US

Tanith Belbin
@TanithJLB
Followers: 2,297
US

Rachael Flatt
@RachaelFlatt
Followers: 1,359
US

Emily Hughes
@EmHughes26
Followers: 1,287
US

Joannie Rochette
@JoannieRochette
Followers: 1,425
Canada

Evan Lysacek
@EvanLysacek
Followers: 1,365
US

Ashley Wagner
@AshWagner2010
Followers: 1,083
US

Kimmie Meissner
@kimmiemeissner
Followers: 2,267
US

Johnny Weir
@JohnnyGWeir
Followers: 3,772
US

Melissa Gregory & Denis Petukhov
@OlympianUncut
Followers: 7,468
US

Michael Weiss
@MichaelWeiss2
Followers: 479
US

Adam Rippon
@Adaripp
Followers: 2,615
US

Charlie White
@CharlieAWhite
Followers: 960
US

Football (NFL)

Troy Aikman
@Troy_Aikman
Followers: 158,882
Retired, Dallas Cowboys, Quarterback

Cliff Avril
@cliffavril
Followers: 2,235
Detroit Lions, Defensive End

Celebrity Tweets
"People talk about finding their lives. In reality, your life is not something you find - it's something you create." David Phillips
@BJRTH (Walter Jones)

Champ Bailey
@champbailey
Followers: 25,889
Denver Broncos, Cornerback

Nate Burleson
@Nate81Burleson
Followers: 5,456
Seattle Seahawks, Wide Receiver

Ramses Barden
@rbarden11
Followers: 2,466
New York Giants, Wide Receiver

Reggie Bush
@reggie_bush
Followers: 611,706
New Orleans Saints, Running Back

Nick Barnett
@NickBarnett
Followers: 165,212
Green Bay Packers, Linebacker

James Casey
@jamescasey86
Followers: 1,255
Houston Texans, Tight End

Celebrity Tweets
How about Brett Farve last night I mean, he is 40 years old and can still throw the ball harder than anybody in the NFL. What a Legend!!!!
@clarence_vaughn (Clarence Vaughn)

Drew Bennett
@DrewBennett83
Followers: 640
Baltimore Ravens, Wide Receiver

Nate Clements
@NateClements
Followers: 6,716
San Francisco 49ers, Cornerback

Celebrity Tweets
Is it me or do the Lakers always seem like they are playing at home for some reason? Do they any away games? Lol
@kirkmorrison52 (Kirk Morrison)

Drew Brees
@drewbrees
Followers: 36,035
New Orleans Saints, Quarterback

Josh Cribbs
@JoshCribbs16
Followers: 4,806
Cleveland Browns, Wide Receiver

Lomas Brown
@LomasBrown75
Followers: 433
Retired, Detroit Lions, Offensive Lineman

Aaron Curry
@SeaHawk59
Followers: 9,904
Seattle Seahawks, Linebacker

Jay Cutler
@JayCutler6
Followers: 31,815
Chicago Bears, Quarterback

Keith Eloi
@KeithEloi
Followers: 891
Washington Redskins, Wide Receiver

Celebrity Tweets
wow mark herzlich is a true beast and a example of a miracle at work (beating Cancer). gave me goose bumps.
@Jonathanstewar1 (Jonathan Stewart)

Vernon Davis
@VernonDavis85
Followers: 14,266
San Francisco 49ers, Tight End

Lee Evans
@leeevans83
Followers: 4,824
Buffalo Bills, Wide Receiver

Marcus Dixon
@marcusdixon92
Followers: 1,386
Dallas Cowboys, Defensive End

Brett Favre
@RealBrettFavre4
Followers: 1,194
Minnesota Vikings, Quarterback

Celebrity Tweets
More Hawks wit MoHawks! The hairstyle took over our team!
@Nate81Burleson (Nate Burleson)

Kevin Dockery
@treyfive
Followers: 1,210
New York Giants, Cornerback

Larry Fitzgerald
@Lfitzgerald11
Followers: 221,090
Arizona Cardinals, Wide Receiver

Darnell Dockett
@ddockett
Followers: 15,608
Arizona Cardinals, Defensive End

Nick Folk
@nickfolk6
Followers: 745
Dallas Cowboys, Kicker

Braylon Edwards
@OfficialBraylon
Followers: 10,619
New York Jets, Wide Receiver

Justin Forsett
@JForsett
Followers: 3,913
Seattle Seahawks, Running Back

Celebrity Tweets
just began hot yoga...98 degrees! Back 2 back days and I'm sore but not sure why. Trying 2 decide whether to keep up with it. Whatcha think?
@Troy_Aikman (Troy Aikman)

Matt Forte
@chitownforte22
Followers: 24,364
Chicago Bears, Running Back

Matthew Hasselbeck
@MatthewHass8
Followers: 19,211
Seattle Seahawks, Quarterback

Celebrity Tweets
I find it odd that my days off are consistently turning into my busiest and most productive days, parents wud be proud. dang, that reminds me.
@rbarden11 (Ramses Barden)

David Garrard
@davidgarrard9
Followers: 3,935
Jacksonville Jaguars, Quarterback

Priest Holmes
@priestholmes
Followers: 3,116
Retired, Kansas City Chiefs, Running Back

Cody Glenn
@txhusker34
Followers: 378
Indianapolis Colts, Linebacker

Santonio Holmes
@santonio10
Followers: 3,719
Pittsburgh Steelers, Wide Receiver

Celebrity Tweets
We're in Scottsdale-- there is this big orange thing in the sky-- looks familiar. I think they call it the sun.
@MatthewHass8 (Matthew Hasselbeck)

Ryan Grant
@RyanGrant25
Followers: 20,347
Green Bay Packers, Running Back

Corvey Irvin
@CorveyIrvin
Followers: 477
Carolina Panthers, Defensive Tackle

Caleb Hanie
@CalebHanie12
Followers: 2,581
Chicago Bears, Quarterback

Malcolm Jenkins
@MalcolmJenkins
Followers: 7,308
New Orleans Saints, Cornerback

Celebrity Tweets
Can anybody tell me what's the most realistic fishing game on wii?
@Txhusker34 (Cody Glenn)

Chris Johnson
@ChrisJohnson28
Followers: 31,521
Tennessee Titans, Running Back

Aaron Maybin
@AaronMaybin58
Followers: 8,692
Buffalo Bills, Defensive End

Derrick Johnson
@superdj56
Followers: 2,267
Kansas City Chiefs, Linebacker

Bryant McKinnie
@bigmacvikings
Followers: 7,204
Minnesota Vikings, Offensive Tackle

Walter Jones
@BJRTH
Followers: 4,369
Seattle Seahawks, Offensive Tackle

Lawyer Milloy
@LawyerMilloy
Followers: 1,534
Seattle Seahawks, Safety

Maurice Jones-Drew
@Jones_Drew32
Followers: 26,011
Jacksonville Jaguars, Running Back

Kenny Moore
@KennyMoore81
Followers: 826
Carolina Panthers, Wide Receiver

Ray Lewis
@raylewis52com
Followers: 4,814
Baltimore Ravens, Linebacker

Knowshon Moreno
@knowshonmoreno
Followers: 11,884
Denver Broncos, Running Back

Celebrity Tweets
the game today is gonna be like Ali n Holmes, Brown n Rihanna, Houston n Bobby Brown<--none of that makes sense? Huh
@OGOchoCinco (Chad Ochocinco)

Payton Manning
@18PeytonManning
Followers: 1,937
Indianapolis Colts, Quarterback

Kirk Morrison
@kirkmorrison52
Followers: 154,866
Oakland Raiders, Linebacker

Randy Moss
@r81m
Followers: 29,809
New England Patriots, Wide Receiver

Sinorice Moss
@Humble83
Followers: 12,334
New York Giants, Wide Receiver

Chad Ochocinco
@OGOchoCinco
Followers: 401,246
Cincinnati Bengals, Wide Receiver

Terrell Owens
@terrellowens
Followers: 244,743
Buffalo Bills, Wide Receiver

Roscoe Parrish
@scoe11
Followers: 2,786
Buffalo Bills, Wide Receiver

Mike Peterson
@mikepeterson53
Followers: 764
Atlanta Falcons, Linebacker

Kerry Rhodes
@kerryrhodes
Followers: 168,449
New York Jets, Free Safety

Antrel Rolle
@antrelrolle
Followers: 2,845
Arizona Cardinals, Free Safety

Warren Sapp
@QBKILLA
Followers: 198,528
Retired, Oakland Raiders, Defensive Tackle

Lydell Sargeant
@lsarge10
Followers: 1,205
Buffalo Bills, Defensive Back

Gerald Sensabaugh
@Gsensabaugh
Followers: 1,856
Dallas Cowboys, Safety

Kory Sheets
@Sheets24K
Followers: 1,117
Miami Dolphins, Running Back

Celebrity Tweets

Sitting outside on rocking chairs and just listening to the sounds of New Orleans from the front porch is pretty cool. The simple things.
@drewbrees (Drew Brees)

Tutan Reyes
@tutanreyes
Followers: 1,112
Houston Texans, Offensive Lineman

Steve Slaton
@ThaDoubleS
Followers: 10,124
Houston Texans, Running Back

Sports

Antonio Smith
@antoniosmith94
Followers: 1,104
Houston Texans, Defensive End

Michael Strahan
@michaelstrahan
Followers: 170,748
Retired, New York Giants, Defensive End

Emmitt Smith
@EmmittSmith22
Followers: 3,268
Retired, Dallas Cowboys, Running Back

Thurman Thomas
@thurmanthomas
Followers: 3,186
Retired, Miami Dolphins, Running Back

Marcus Spears
@mspear96
Followers: 3,484
Dallas Cowboys, Defensive End

Pierre Thomas
@Pierre_Thomas
Followers: 8,607
New Orleans Saints, Running Back

Takeo Spikes
@TakeoSpikes51
Followers: 147,434
San Francisco 49ers, Linebacker

Chip Vaughn
@ChipVaughn
Followers: 1,615
New Orleans Saints, Safety

Joe Staley
@jstaley74
Followers: 3,026
San Francisco 49ers, Offensive Tackle

Clarence Vaughn
@clarence_vaughn
Followers: 452
Retired, Washington Redskins, Safety

Jonathan Stewart
@Jonathanstewar1
Followers: 7,185
Carolina Panthers, Running Back

Hines Ward
@HWmvp86
Followers: 7,477
Pittsburgh Steelers, Wide Receiver

Celebrity Tweets

quote of the week: make yourself indispensable and you'll be moved up. Act as if you're indispensable and you'll be moved out -jules ormont

@NateClements (Nate Clements)

Fabian Washington
@FABEWASH31
Followers: 5,770
Baltimore Ravens, Cornerback

Damien Woody
@damienwoody
Followers: 1,556
New York Jets, Tackle

Chandler Williams
@Chandler18
Followers: 874
Free Agent, Wide Receiver

Golf (LPGA/PGA)

Stuart Appleby
@StuartAppleby
Followers: 5,891
8 time tour winner

Paul Casey
@Paul_Casey
Followers: 16,416
Ranked 3rd in the world

Rich Beem
@Richbeem
Followers: 760
Won 2002 Championship

Stewart Cink
@stewartcink
Followers: 1,081,329
Won 2009 Open

Notah Begay III
@NotahBegay3
Followers: 2,148
Only Native American on Tour

Paula Creamer
@ThePCreamer
Followers: 2,413
Nicknamed The Pink Panther

Celebrity Tweets

Interesting to see couples in Korea wearing the same shirt/sweater. Exactly the same shirt! I heard its very now! Hmmmm not my cup of tea.

@TheAnnaRawson (Anna Rowson)

Sports

Celebrity Tweets
A great and historic day for the game of golf! Moments ago, the IOC voted that golf (as well as rugby) would be added to the 2016 Olympics.
@jacknicklaus (Jack Nicklaus)

John Daly
@PGA_JohnDaly
Followers: 35,158
Nicknamed Long John

Peter Jacobsen
@JakeTrout
Followers: 3,959
Played himself in Tin Cup

Chris DiMarco
@ChrisDiMarco
Followers: 10,783
Norma DiMarco Tee Up For Life

Christina Kim
@TheChristinaKim
Followers: 6,396
Animated, vocal player

Rickie Fowler
@RickieFowlerPGA
Followers: 1,372
Ranked 1st in the world for 36 weeks

J.L. Lewis
@JLLewisGolf
Followers: 302
Won 1999 John Deere Classic

Celebrity Tweets
As usual, lot of media requests and a lot of autographs to sign, but all fun & enjoying every day. Just one thing. I prefer being called YE
@Y_E_Yang (Y.E. Yang)

Tadd Fujikawa
@Tadd_Fujikawa
Followers: 2,456
Youngest golfer to qualify for the Open

Davis Love III
@Love3d
Followers: 14,593
Every Shot I Take

Celebrity Tweets
Proud of Mickelson for winning the Tour Championship after what he and his family have gone through this year. Well deserved!
@JakeTrout (Peter Jacobsen)

Trevor Immelman
@TrevorImmelman
Followers: 5,788
Won 2008 Masters

Paige Mackenzie
@Paige_Mackenzie
Followers: 2,481
University of Washington

Hunter Mahan

@HunterMahan

Followers: 2,713

Captain of the US team

Geoff Ogilvy

@geoffogilvy

Followers: 8,503

Won 2006 Open

Celebrity Tweets

ok I'll share a fun bit we're doin---I'm hittin balls with my Adams driver off the roof of my bus

@PGA_JohnDaly (John Daly)

Rory McIlroy

@Rorsmcilroy

Followers: 15,686

The most exciting young player in the world

Pat Perez

@PatPerezGolf

Followers: 2,425

Won 2009 Bob Hope Classic

Celebrity Tweets

I sign up and off I go. It's an interesting medium for communication and sharing info. The world has changed a lot from the fax machine.

StuartAppleby (Stuart Appleby)

Parker McLachlin

@ParkerMcLachlin

Followers: 2,559

Cited for tweeting during a tournament

Suzann Pettersen

@suzannpettersen

Followers: 5,727

Member of European League

Kristy McPherson

@KRISTY2208

Followers: 2,701

The Big Break VI

Ian Poulter

@Ianjamespoulter

Followers: 820,734

Radical dresser

Celebrity Tweets

Stopped at Shell station to gas up @lisacink's car. Across the street--another Shell station. Go figure that strategy!

@stewartcink (Stewart Cink)

Jack Nicklaus

@jacknicklaus

Followers: 867

Nicknamed The Golden Bear

Morgan Pressel

@morganpressel

Followers: 12,893

Girls Rolex Junior Player of the Year

Anna Rawson
@TheAnnaRawson
Followers: 5,961
Australian, model

Thomas Brent Weekley
@booweekley
Followers: 4,162
Nicknamed Boo Boo Bear

Annika Sorenstam
@ANNIKA59
Followers: 7,364
2003 Golf World Hall of Fame

Michelle Wie
@themichellewie
Followers: 11,272
Amateur player at age 10

Celebrity Tweets
Caddies + free beer = someone is getting a wrong yardage tomorrow.
@Paul_Casey (Paul Casey)

Kevin Streelman
@Streels54
Followers: 524
Does not fly to tournaments

Oliver Wilson
@Oliver_Wilson
Followers: 1,673
Rookie season 2005

Stan Utley
@stanutley
Followers: 625
Top 50 greatest golf teachers

Tiger Woods
@tigerwoods
Followers: 6,952
Ranked 1st in the world

Camilo Villegas
@CamiloVillegasR
Followers: 12,615
Won a grand slam at 16

Y.E. Yang
@Y_E_Yang
Followers: 1,161
Won 2009 PGA Championship

Celebrity Tweets
Making a vanilla latte with the new espresso machine. Watch out Starbucks !!
@ANNIKA59 (Annika Sorenstam)

Bubba Watson
@bubbawatson
Followers: 5,316
Longest drive, 398 yards

Hockey (NHL)

Colby Armstrong
@armdog
Followers: 948
Atlanta Thrashers

Dan Ellis
@dellis39
Followers: 1,000
Nashville Predators

Dan Boyle
@danboyle22
Followers: 3,848
San Jose Sharks

Bruno Gervais
@BGervais8
Followers: 864
New York Islanders

Celebrity Tweets
Favorite moment of my career so far? My 1st NHL game.
@Martinhavlat (Martin Havla)

Donald Brashear
@dbrashear87
Followers: 1,407
New York Rangers

Mike Green
@GreenLife52
Followers: 3,088
Washington Capitals

Mike Commodore
@commie22
Followers: 1,854
Columbus Blue Jackets

Martin Havla
@martinhavlat
Followers: 14,085
Minnesota Wild

Riley Cote
@rileecoyote
Followers: 2,334
Philadelphia Flyers

Alex Ovechkin
@ovi8
Followers: 25,950
Washington Capitals

Patrik Elias
@pelias
Followers: 6,121
New Jersey Devils

David Perron
@DP_57
Followers: 2,781
St. Louis Blues

Sports

Alexander Steen
@a10steen
Followers: 907
St. Louis Blues

Brendan Witt
@BWitt32
Followers: 970
New York Islanders

Celebrity Tweets
At DC airport with tons of obama fans. Taking a 1 day vacation to relax - I'll have more from mtl tomorrow
@ovi8 (Alex Ovechkin)

Kevin Weekes
@KevinWeekes
Followers: 3,318
New Jersey Devils

Olympic Medalists

Dorothy Hamill
@DorthyHamill
Followers: 502
Figure skater

Nastia Liukin
@NLiukin
Followers: 19,831
Gymnast

Celebrity Tweets
A little freaky how dead on my horoscopes have been.... I think the world is trying to talk to me.
@NLiukin (Nastia Liukin)

Shawn Johnson
@ShawneyJ
Followers: 48,653
Gymnast

Apolo Anton Ohno
@ApoloOhno
Followers: 3,932
Speed skater

Celebrity Tweets
What a day…much to short of a stay in Seattle but I must get back to prep for 2010 Games. Thanks to all who came to the event today!
@ApoloOhno (Apolo Anton Ohno)

Michael Phelps
@Michael_Phelps
Followers: 41,797
Swimmer

Kristi Yamaguchi
@yamaguchikristi
Followers: 3,203
Figure skater

Celebrity Tweets
"The most important thing is to enjoy your life—to be happy—it's all that matters." —
Audrey Hepburn -from a follower... I love it
@ShawneyJ (Shawn Johnson)

Shaun White
@Shaun_White
Followers: 50,503
Professional snowboarder

Skiing

Ingrid Backstrom
@ingridbackstrom
Followers: 1,126
US

Ian Cosco
@chuggLIFE
Followers: 340
Canada

Rory Bushfield
@Bushywayne
Followers: 504
Canada

Simon Dumont
@SimonDumont06
Followers: 931
US

Sammy Carlson
@SammyCskiing
Followers: 601
US

Tim Durtschi
@TimDurtschi
Followers: 363
US

Emily Cook
@emilycook
Followers: 329
US

Grete Eliassen
@greteeliassen
Followers: 924
US

Sports

Fredrik Ericsson
@fredrikericsson
Followers: 263
France

Tanner Hall
@TannerHall
Followers: 2,187
US

Alex Harvey
@alex_harvey
Followers: 277
US

Andrew Hathaway
@hathbanger
Followers: 636
US

Henrik Lampert
@HankLambo
Followers: 271
US

Ted Ligety
@tedligety
Followers: 810
US

Nick Martini
@NicholasMartini
Followers: 484
US

Bode Miller
@olympicskier
Followers: 394
US

Johnny Moseley
@jonnymoseley
Followers: 2,170
US

Nick Nerbonne
@NickNerbonne
Followers: 535
US

Shaun Palmer
@Palmer555
Followers: 463
US

Michelle Parker
@MyshellParker
Followers: 579
US

Daron Rahlves
@DRahlves
Followers: 597
US

Maelle Ricker
@Maelle_Ricker
Followers: 1,202
Canada

TJ Schiller
@tjschiller
Followers: 1,197
Canada

Aksel Lund Svindal
@akselsvindal
Followers: 2,684
Norway

Kaya Turski
@**kayaturski**
Followers: 361
Canada

Tom Wallisch
@**TWallisch**
Followers: 891
US

Lindsey Vonn
@**lindseyvonn**
Followers: 2,267
US

Soccer

Freddy Adu
@**FreddyAdu11**
Followers: 159,674
Belenenses

Joe Cannon
@**josephrcannon**
Followers: 529
San Jose Earthquakes

DaMarcus Beasley
@**DaMarcusBeasley**
Followers: 4,887
Rangers

Michael Chabala
@**Chabala17**
Followers: 1,078
Houston Dynamo

Celebrity Tweets
"How am I going to live today in order to create the tomorrow I'm committed to?" —
Tony Robbins: Self-help speaker and author
@**angelahucles (Angela Hucles)**

Jim Brennan
@**jimmybrennan**
Followers: 549
Toronto FC

Brandi Chastain
@**brandichastain**
Followers: 1,253
FC Gold Pride

Edson Buddle
@**EdsonBuddle**
Followers: 788
Los Angeles Galaxy

Brian Ching
@**brianching**
Followers: 5,357
Houston Dynamo

Sports

Danny Cruz
@Cruz05
Followers: 928
Houston Dynamo

Alecko Eskandarian
@alecko11
Followers: 1,487
Los Angeles Galaxy

Charlie Davies
@CharlieDavies9
Followers: 13,207
French Ligue

Hunter Freeman
@huntfree
Followers: 254
IK Start

Jonathan De Guzman
@jdeguz
Followers: 1,272
Dutch Eredivisie club Feyenoord

Brad Guzan
@bguzan
Followers: 3,772
Aston Villa

Celebrity Tweets

Getting super excited for the Mad Men premier....love me some 60s ad execs and secretary style
@alywagner (Aly Wagner)

Dwayne DeRosario
@dwaynederosario
Followers: 2,859
Toronto FC

Stuart Holden
@stuholden22
Followers: 8,389
Houston Dynamo

Danny Dichio
@DannyDichio
Followers: 4,101
Toronto FC Academy coach

Angela Hucles
@angelahucles
Followers: 414
US Women's National Soccer Team

Robert Earnshaw
@robertearnshaw
Followers: 1,110
Nottingham Forest

Bryan Jordan
@BJ6
Followers: 517
Los Angeles Galaxy

Maurice Edu
@MauriceEdu
Followers: 161,882
Rangers

Kei Kamara
@keikamara
Followers: 752
Kansas City Wizards

Dan Kennedy
@1DanKennedy
Followers: 320
Chivas USA

Sacha Kljestan
@SachaKljestan
Followers: 4,422
Chivas USA

Brad Knighton
@bbknighton
Followers: 269
New England Revolution

Christine Latham
@christinelatham
Followers: 188
Boston Breakers

Karina LeBlanc
@karinaleblanc
Followers: 447
Los Angeles Sol

Freddie Ljungberg
@TheRealFreddie
Followers: 1,085
Seattle Sounders FC

Manya Makoski
@Makoski22
Followers: 158
Los Angeles Sol

Bryan Namoff
@NAMOFF
Followers: 983
DC United

Joseph Ngwenya
@jngwenya
Followers: 293
Antalyaspor

Heath Pearce
@HeathPearce24
Followers: 837
FC Dallas

Michael Petke
@petkemike
Followers: 353
New York Red Bulls

Rohan Ricketts
@rohanricketts
Followers: 1,536
Toronto FC

Robbie Rogers
@robbierogers
Followers: 2,511
Columbus Crew

Alex Scott
@Alexscott2
Followers: 718
Boston Breakers

Celebrity Tweets
Whatd the 5 fingers say to the face? SLAP hahaa Watching old episodes of The Chappelle Show...did u guys used to watch it? Love that show
@MauriceEdu (Maurice Edu)

Sports

Kelly Smith
@kjs8eng
Followers: 1,065
Boston Breakers

Aly Wagner
@alywagner
Followers: 1,146
Los Angeles Sol

Lindsay Tarpley
@lindsaytarpley
Followers: 903
Chicago Red Stars

Tiffany Weimer
@TiffanyWeimer
Followers: 124
Boston Breakers

Chris Tierney
@ChrisTierney8
Followers: 401
New England Revolution

Andy Williams
@bommadog
Followers: 230
Real Salt Lake

Taylor Twellman
@TaylorTwellman
Followers: 1,509
New England Revolution

Chris Wingert
@wingert17
Followers: 266
Real Salt Lake

Tennis

Sabine Lisicki
@sabinelisicki
Followers: 2,327
Ranked 22nd in the world

Andy Roddick
@andyroddick
Followers: 145,680
One of the fastest serves in tennis

Andy Murray
@andy_murray
Followers: 105,800
Ranked 4th in the world

Serena Williams
@serenajwilliams
Followers: 1,364,727
Ranked 1st in the world

Celebrity Tweets
I can't relax I am ironing bed sheets and shams, pillows are going to be ironed next!!!!
Lol never told u that I love ironing!!!!
@serenajwilliams (Serena Williams)

Celebrity Tweets
Serena makes the best tacos
@Venuseswilliams (Venus Williams)

Venus Williams
@Venuseswilliams
Followers: 235,541
Ranked 6th in the world

Wrestling (WWE/WWF)

Chris Jericho
@IAmJericho
Followers: 70,164
WWF

Mike Mizanin
@mikethemiz
Followers: 39,929
WWE, "The MIz"

TV Shows (Cable/Network)

The Celebrity Tweet Directory

30 Rock
@nbc30rock
Followers: 6,976
NBC comedy

60 Minutes
@60Minutes
Followers: 11,633
CBS news

ABC News
@ABCNewsNews
Followers: 6,478
ABC news

All My Children
@AMC1970
Followers: 978
ABC soap opera

America's Got Talent
@nbcagt
Followers: 1,792
NBC talent competition

Antiques Road Show
@RoadshowPBS
Followers: 925
PBS antiques appraisers

As The World Turns
@OfficialATWT
Followers: 2,724
CBS soap opera

Big Brother
@BigBrotherWatch
Followers: 1,349
CBS reality show

Celebrity Tweets
Did you miss last night's 30 Rock? Catch up now - the full episode of "Sun Tea" is up at NBC.com!
@nbc30rock (30 Rock)

AMC News
@AMCnews
Followers: 3,174
AMC news

BONES
@BONESonFOX
Followers: 3,644
FOX drama

Celebrity Tweets
Wondering where to send fan mail for some of your favorite Idols? We have the details
@AmericanIdol (American Idol)

American Idol
@AmericanIdol
Followers: 18,358
FOX singing competition

Bored to Death
@boredtodeath
Followers: 2,521
HBO comedy

124

TV Shows (Cable/Network)

Breaking Bad
@BreakingBad_AMC
Followers: 2,126
AMC drama

Chuck
@nbcchuck
Followers: 3,669
NBC dramady

Britian's Got Talent
@britsgotalent09
Followers: 775
BBC talent show

Cold Case
@ColdCase_CBS
Followers: 648
CBS drama

Celebrity Tweets
Google says BONES was the #2 most popular TV Show search in 2009
@BONESonFOX (Bones)

Californication
@SHO_Cali
Followers: 5,404
Showtime drama

Community
@communitynbc
Followers: 1,091
NBC comedy

Celebrity Tweets
The EPA releases a monumental warning on greenhouse gas emissions.
@CBSEveningNews (CBS Evening News)

Castle
@CastleTV
Followers: 1,711
ABC dramady

Cougar Town
@CougarTownRoom
Followers: 743
ABC comedy

CBS Evening News
@CBSEveningNews
Followers: 1,210
CBS news

Dancing with the Stars
@ABC_DWTS
Followers: 14,243
ABC dance competition

CBS Investigates
@CBSInvestigates
Followers: 1,948
CBS investigative news

Dateline NBC
@datelinenbc
Followers: 7,697
NBC investigative news

The Celebrity Tweet Directory

Celebrity Tweets
RT @NatalieAbrams: Chatted with Zach between scenes and he talked in a British accent. "I'm really British, just faking American," he joked.
@nbcchuck (Chuck)

Day One
@nbcdayone
Followers: 232
NBC drama

Days of Our Lives
@nbcdays
Followers: 10,178
NBC soap opera

Dexter
@SHO_Dexter
Followers: 23,780
Showtime drama

Flash Forward
@TheFlashForward
Followers: 2,898
ABC drama

Flashpoint
@Flashpoint_TV
Followers: 1,194
CBS drama

Fox and Friends
@foxandfriends
Followers: 57,947
FOX morning news

Celebrity Tweets
Brady fills Nicole in on the trouble she's caused running away, while Sami copes with the pain of losing a child twice
@nbcdays (Days of Our Lives)

Dollhouse
@DOLLHOUSEonFOX
Followers: 3,431
FOX drama, canceled

Friday Nights Lights
@nbcfnl
Followers: 2,616
NBC drama

Celebrity Tweets
On last night's #FRINGE, the shoreline was littered with bodies hosting a giant squid-like creature. Watch it now
@FRINGEonFOX (Fringe)

Family Guy
@FamilyGuyonFOX
Followers: 134
FOX animated comedy

Fringe
@FRINGEonFOX
Followers: 11,624
FOX drama

Gary Unmarried
@Gary_CBS
Followers: 120
CBS comedy

Hell's Kitchen
@hellskitchenfox
Followers: 3,778
FOX cooking competition

General Hospital
@PortCharles101
Followers: 297
ABC soap opera

Heroes
@heroes
Followers: 19,277
NBC drama

Celebrity Tweets
Today's 'Gary' Moment: Gary's got his Christopher Walken impression down! Hilarious!!
@Gary_CBS (Gary Unmarried)

Glee
@GLEEonFOX
Followers: 68,792
FOX dramady

House
@HOUSEonFOX
Followers: 9,325
FOX drama

Good Morning America
@GMA
Followers: 1,586,052
ABC morning news

Jimmy Kimmel Live
@JimmyKimmelLive
Followers: 17,334
ABC late night

Celebrity Tweets
I'm loving this elevator scene where Mary McDonnell gives Chandra a taste of her own medicine.
@ABCGreysAnatomy (Grey's Anatomy)

Grey's Anatomy
@ABCGreysAnatomy
Followers: 17,309
ABC drama

Last Call with Carson Daly
@lastcallcd
Followers: 144
NBC late night

HBO Real Sports
@HBORealSports
Followers: 614
HBO sports

Late Night with Jimmy Fallon
@LateNightJimmy
Followers: 24,040
NBC late night

Late Show with David Letterman
@Late_Night
Followers: 9,700
CBS late night

Law and Order
@nbclawandorder
Followers: 1,930
NBC drama

Law and Order: SVU
@nbcsvu
Followers: 8,909
NBC drama

Let's Make a Deal
@LetsMakeDealCBS
Followers: 26
CBS game show

Mad Men
@MadMen_AMC
Followers: 9,466
AMC drama

Medium
@Medium_CBS
Followers: 428
CBS drama

Mercy
@nbcmercy
Followers: 399
NBC drama

MLB on FOX
@MLBONFOX
Followers: 18,252
Fox baseball

Celebrity Tweets
Happy to share that Benjamin Bratt will guest star in our December 4 episode = get excited for the return of Det. Curtis!
@nbclawandorder (Law and Order)

Lie To Me
@LieToMeScoop
Followers: 1,253
FOX drama

Lock 'N Load
@SHO_Locknload
Followers: 47
Showtime reality

Lost
@Lost_on_ABC
Followers: 72,720
ABC drama

NBC Nightly News
@nbcnightlynews
Followers: 16,118
NBC evening news

NBC Sports
@nbc_sports
Followers: 12,056
NBC sports

NCIS
@NCIS_CBS
Followers: 11,487
CBS/USA drama

TV Shows (Cable/Network)

NCIS LA
@NCISLA_CBS
Followers: 2,969
CBS drama

One Life to Live
@OLTLInsider
Followers: 1,386
ABC soap opera

NFL on FOX
@NFLONFOX
Followers: 26,454
FOX football

Parks and Recreation
@parksandrecnbc
Followers: 9,000
NBC comedy

Nightline
@Nightline
Followers: 1,420,074
ABC late night news

Private Practice
@PP_Scoop
Followers: 992
ABC drama

NPR Weekend
@NPRWeekend
Followers: 7,423
NPR weekend news

Real Time with Bill Maher
@RealBillMaher
Followers: 817
HBO talk show

Numb3rs
@Numb3rs_CBS
Followers: 793
CBS drama

Saturday Night Live
@nbcsnl
Followers: 17,587
NBC comedy

Scrubs
@scrubs
Followers: 9,361
ABC comedy

Survivor
@Survivor_Tweet
Followers: 3,408
CBS survival competition

Celebrity Tweets
After another dramatic blindside last night, another Survivor is sent packing to Ponderosa... Watch Now!
@Survivor_Tweet (Survivor)

Southland
@SouthlandNBC
Followers: 368
TNT drama

Writers

Diablo Cody
@diablcody
Followers: 113,581
Juno, Jennifer's Body

Caroline Myss
@caroline_myss
Followers: 3,564
Defy Gravity…

Paul Cornell
@Paul_Cornell
Followers: 5,036
Doctor Who, Captain Britain

Suze Orman
@SuzeOrmanShow
Followers: 938,354
Suze Orman's 2009 Action Plan…

Stephenie Meyer
@Stephenie_Meyer
Followers: 8,451
Twilight series

Jimmy Palmiotti
@jpalmiotti
Followers: 2,854
Power Girl series

Celebrity Tweets
Unbelievable Seattle signing. My favorite of the tour. Sonics fans showed up in force. STILL AN NBA CITY. Thanks to everyone.
@sportsguy33 (Bill Simmons)

Linda Lael Miller
@lindalaelmiller
Followers: 231
The Bridgroom, State Secrets

Steven Pressfield
@SPressfield
Followers: 1,634
The Legend of Bagger Vance

Greg Mortenson
@gregmortenson
Followers: 5,560
Three Cups of Tea…

Shonda Rhimes
@shondarhimes
Followers: 22,856
Grey's Anatomy, Private Practice

Celebrity Tweets
However, I should flag up now that although I could twitter endlessly, I'm afraid you won't be hearing from me very often…
@jk_rowling (J K Rowling)

Chip Mosher
@chipmosher
Followers: 142
Left on Mission, Silicon Towers

Anne Rice
@AnneRiceAuthor
Followers: 7,427
The Vampire Chronicles

Celebrity Tweets

CougarTown guys sent cookies cuz I tweeted I liked their show. Free cookies for no reason! From nice guys! Watching TV DOES have perks!

@Shondarhimes (Shonda Rhimes)

Cheryl Richardson

@coachoncall

Followers: 6,750

Take Time for Your Life

Andrew Ross Sorkin

@andrewrsorkin

Followers: 101,100

Too Big to Fail…

Celebrity Tweets

Educating girls is the key to peace. BYU University rocks!

@Gregmortenson (Greg Mortenson)

JK Rowling

@jk_rowling

Followers: 85,742

Harry Potter series

Danielle Steel

@daniellesteel

Followers: 99

Southern Lights: a Novel

Brandon Sanderson

@BrandonSandrson

Followers: 4,547

Mistborn trilogy

Elizabeth Strout

@ElizStrout

Followers: 148

Olive Kitteridge

Bill Simmons

@sportsguy33

Followers: 1,007,084

The Book of Basketball

Eckhart Tolle

@Eckhart_Tolle

Followers: 7,524

The Power of Now, A New Earth

Celebrity Tweets

You've not yet even scratched the surface of what you're capable of. Your potential is beyond your wildest imagining.

@Marwilliamson (Marianne Williamson)

L.J. Smith

@drujienna

Followers: 946

The Vampire Diaries

Dr. Andrew Weil

@DrWeil

Followers: 4,583

Why Our Health Matters…

The Celebrity Tweet Directory

Celebrity Tweets
Intuition is natural by-product of flowering of a mature self-esteem and a sense of empowerment – not power over, but power to be
@caroline_myss (Caroline Myss)

Jack Welch

@jack_welch
Followers: 1,034,949
Winning

Bill Willingham

@BillWillingham
Followers: 1,181
Fables series

Celebrity Tweets
Challenge: Make eye contact and smile at strangers all day long :-)
@Coachoncall (Cheryl Richardson)

Marianne Williamson

@marwilliamson
Followers: 20,314
A Return to Love

How Do I follow Other Twitter Users?

Twitter would be just another lonely outpost on the fringes of the Web if all anyone ever did was post tweets. Twitter is, instead, a vibrant, noisy place because it goes beyond mere microblogging and embraces its social side by letting you follow other tweeters. This means that you subscribe to that person's updates, which then appear on your home page, so you can easily keep track of what that person shares with the Twitterverse. By following your pals, family, colleagues, and even total strangers that you find inexplicably fascinating, and by replying to tweets, exchanging messages with your friends, and sending friends' tweets to your followers, you begin to get the full measure of the Twitter experience.

finding People

As you see a bit later, to follow someone on Twitter, you must usually access that person's Twitter page. That's fine and all, but how do you find someone's page? If you don't know anyone on Twitter (or, probably more accurately, if you haven't yet discovered people you know on Twitter), how do you find someone to follow? Fortunately, Twitter offers a number of features that make it fairly easy to find people you know or people who are worth following. The next few sections provide the details.

finding people with Twitter accounts

The best way to get started is to use the Find on Twitter feature, which enables you to scour the database of tweeters for someone you know. You can search by first name, last name, or even the person's Twitter username. Here's how it works:

1. **Sign in to your Twitter account.**
2. **Click Find People.** The Find People page appears.
3. **Click the Find on Twitter tab.**
4. **Use the text box to type the name (first or last or both) of the person you're looking for.** Using both first and last names is usually the way to go here. If that doesn't work, use just the last name or the first name, whichever is more unique. If all you have is a partial username, you can enter that instead.
5. **In the search results, click the person's avatar or username to check out their profile.**

finding someone on another network

Searching for the members of your posse individually using the Find on Twitter feature is an easy way to get going, but it can be time-consuming and frustrating if you keep coming up empty. An often better way to go is to get Twitter to do some of the legwork for you. Specifically, you can tell Twitter to rummage through your list of contacts on your Gmail, Yahoo!, or AOL account. If Twitter finds one or more tweeters, it displays them in a list.

Follow these steps to give this a whirl:

1. **Sign in to your Twitter account.**
2. **Click Find People.** The Find People page appears.
3. **Click the Find on other networks tab.**
4. **Click the network you want to scour: Gmail, Yahoo!, or AOL.**
5. **Type the e-mail address and password for that account, as shown in figure A.**

Caution

If you feel a bit queasy at the thought of handing over your account credentials to Twitter, then good for you for having some security common sense. Many social networking services offer a similar feature, and you should never dole out third-party login data willy-nilly. Check the site's privacy policy, and only provide your credentials if you trust the site.

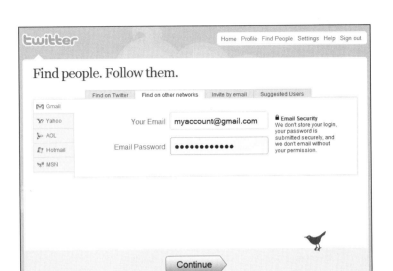

A Choose your network and then enter your login credentials.

6. **Click Continue.** Twitter connects to your account, downloads your contacts list, and then checks for matches in the Twitter database. If it finds any, it displays them in a list and selects the check box beside each person by default.

7. **If there are any people you don't want to follow, deselect the check box beside each of those people.**

8. **Click Follow.** Twitter displays the Why not invite some friends? page, which lists all your contacts who don't have a Twitter account. You can use this list to extend invitations to one or more contacts to join Twitter.

9. **Select the check box beside each person you want to invite.**

10. **Click Invite.** Twitter fires off an e-mail message to each person.

Inviting someone to join Twitter

Many people enjoy Twitter so much that they want to share the experience with their close friends, respected co-workers, and the saner members of their family. Other tweeters have a hard time finding anyone they know on Twitter, so it becomes a bit of a lonely place. Whichever camp you find yourself in, you can share Twitter with people you know by sending them an e-mail invitation to join the service. The message that Twitter sends on your behalf looks like this:

The Celebrity Tweet Directory

From: Your Name Here
Subject: Your Name Here wants to keep up with you on Twitter
To find out more about Twitter, visit the link below:
http://twitter.com/i/0f6fc06f0d52c55f25246b7316ea81c5324564a6

Thanks,
-The Twitter Team

About Twitter

Twitter is a unique approach to communication and networking based on the simple concept of status. With Twitter, you may answer this question over SMS or the Web and the responses are shared between contacts.

When your friends click the link, they see your Twitter profile page with a link to join up.

If this sounds like a plan, follow these steps to send out the invitations:

1. **Sign in to your Twitter account.**

2. **Click Find People.** The Find People page appears.

3. **Click the Invite by email tab.**

4. **Use the large text box to type the e-mail address of the person you want to invite.** If you want to fire off multiple invites, separate each address with a comma, as shown in figure B.

5. **Click Invite.** Twitter dispatches an e-mail message to each address.

B Choose your network and then enter your login credentials.

Tracking FollowFriday recommendations

Following people you know is a big part of Twitter's appeal, and it adds an irresistible personal touch to the service. However, although I'm sure your friends and family are fascinating, it's a vast Twitterverse, and it's teeming with smart, funny, engaging people whose tweets just might improve your day if you followed them. But how on earth do you find these people? The best way is by asking the tweeters you do know for suggestions. Just post an update asking your followers who they recommend, and then check out the resulting tweeters as the responses come in. (In any Twitter post, if you see @ followed by a username, you can click that username to view the person's profile.)

Tip

A more indirect way to canvass your followers is to check out who they follow. On your home or profile page, click the Followers link, click a username, and then click the person's Following link. I've found perhaps a third of the people I follow using this method.

That should get you a few good recommendations, but why stop at just your followers when you can get the entire Twitosphere involved? Well, perhaps not everyone, but at least every tweeter who knows about FollowFridays. This is a Twitter topic where every Friday people post one or more updates that recommend a particularly good tweeter. Each update includes the #followfriday hashtag, so all FollowFridays are easily found and searched. Here are a couple of ways you can track FollowFriday updates:

- **Use Twitter search.** You can use Twitter's advanced search feature to search for a particular hashtag. However, for now you can plug the following address into your Web browser: http://twitter.com/#search?q=%23followfriday.

- **Use TopFollowFriday.** This site tracks the most endorsed tweeters, either on the current day or all-time: http://topfollowfriday.com/.

Following People

The best way to revel in another person's Twitter goodness is to follow that person. Sure, you can simply use your Web browser to dial up a person's Twitter profile and read their stuff, but you lose the immediacy of seeing their updates arrive in your timeline, and you miss out on some of the social aspects of Twitter (such as not being able to send a message directly to that person).

following someone on Twitter

Following someone on Twitter usually takes just a single click, but what you click depends on where you are in the Twitter interface. There are two possibilities:

- **Viewing a person's profile page.** In this case, look for the Follow button under the person's avatar. Twitter replaces the Follow button with a Following notice, as shown in figure C.

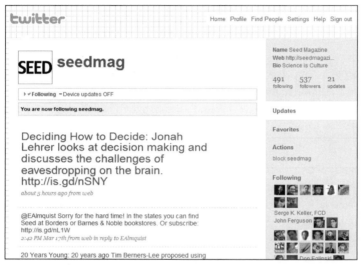

C In a tweeter's profile page, click the Follow link and Twitter changes your status to Following.

- **Viewing a list of followers or friends.** In this case, each tweeter in the list has a Follow button, and you click that button to follow that person. Twitter removes the Follow button and displays You are now following *username* (where *username* is the person's Twitter screen name), as shown in figure D.

D In a list of followers or friends, click a tweeter's Follow link and Twitter changes your status, as shown here.

note

If instead of a Follow button you see the message This person has protected their updates, it means the user must approve your follow request. Click the Send request button to make the request.

Following Twitter's suggested users

If you're really not sure where to start with this following business, then you might want to take a look at Twitter's Suggested Users page, which lists over 100 Twitter users. The list is a real mixed bag that includes mostly members of the Twitterati (the Twitter elite who have the most followers) — including celebrities, companies, media outlets and personalities, and bands — plus the odd apparently randomly selected tweeter. It's not exactly personal, but it's an easy way to populate your friend timeline.

note

To keep track of the most popular tweeters, check out Twitterholic at http://twitterholic.com.

Here are the steps to follow:

1. **Sign in to your Twitter account.**
2. **Click Find People.** The Find People page appears.
3. **Click the Suggested Users tab.** Twitter displays a list of users.
4. **Select the check box beside each person you want to follow.** Twitter adds the user's avatar under the You'll be following heading, as shown in figure E.
5. **Click Follow.** Twitter returns you to your home page and you see the latest messages from your selected users in your friend timeline.

note

If you want to dive into the deep end, select the Select All check box to select every suggested user.

E In the Suggested Users tab, select the check box beside each user you want to follow.

Understanding verified accounts

Twitter is home to a remarkable number of celebrities. For many people, this is one of the most amazing and unique features of Twitter, because it seems to give you incredible access to the day-to-day lives of the rich and famous. Unfortunately, Twitter is also home to a remarkable number of fake celebrities: accounts that appear to be posting tweets from an honest-to-gosh celeb, but that are actually just the musings of some wannabe in Wilmington.

Twitter doesn't ask for ID when you create an account. If you want to use the name of some famous person as your Twitter moniker, there's nothing stopping you, and hundreds of too-much-time-on-their-hands miscreants have done just that. Until recently, Twitter seemed to more or less be turning a blind eye to these ersatz accounts, but then Tony LaRussa, the manager of baseball's St. Louis Cardinals, decided to sue Twitter because an imposter was posting tweets under his name. That caught Twitter's collective attention in a hurry, and the solution they came up with is the verified account. Basically, if you sign up for a Twitter account and you're famous enough to have people wanting to impersonate you; Twitter HQ will jump through a few extra hoops to ensure you are who you say you are.

Tip

If you're famous, or if you're having problems with someone impersonating you on Twitter, you can request that the Twitter folk verify your account. Fill in the Verified Account form at http://twitter.com/account/verify_request. They may not verify you (as I write this Twitter is verifying only a limited number of accounts), but it doesn't hurt to ask.

Following a person's updates via RSS

If you're a dedicated blog follower and find yourself spending more time in your RSS reader than just about anywhere else, you might not like the idea of having to access the Twitter site or even sign in to your Twitter account to follow a particular person's tweets. Similarly, you might be following someone's tweets and you don't want to miss a thing while you're not signed in to Twitter. In both cases, Twitter makes each user's timeline available in an RSS feed, so you can add that feed to your favorite RSS reader. Twitter even makes it easy to subscribe to the feed using Live Bookmarks, Bloglines, Google, or My Yahoo!. Here's how it works:

1. **Sign in to your Twitter account.** Actually, this part is optional because you don't need to be logged in to access someone's RSS feed. However, if you want to get the feed for one of your friends or followers, then you need to sign in.

2. **Navigate to the user's profile page.**

3. **In the sidebar, click the RSS feed of** *username***'s updates link, where** *username* **is the user's screen name.** Twitter displays the feed, as shown in figure F.

4. **Subscribe to the feed.** The steps required here vary depending on your RSS reader. The standard technique is to copy the feed URL in the browser's address bar, navigate to your RSS service, select the option to add a feed, and then paste the feed address.

F A Twitter user's RSS feed

Tip

If you want to follow all your friends via RSS, sign in, and then click Home to display your friend timeline. In the sidebar, click the RSS feed link and then enter your Twitter login credentials in the dialog box that appears

Following people who follow you

One of the ongoing debates in Twitter circles involves the question of whether you should always follow someone who follows you. Many tweeters believe that it's rude not to follow someone who has been kind enough to sign up for your tweets. After all, that person has indicated they're interested in what you have to say, so by not reciprocating you're effectively saying you're not interested in what they have to say. Not only that, but Twitter's direct message feature (which I discuss in just a bit) requires that two users follow each other. Believe it or not, many Twitter geeks examine a user's *follow ratio*, which compares the number of people that user follows with the number of people that follow the user. A low follow ratio means that a person follows few people compared to how many follow her, and to many tweeters, that's a bad sign.

Other tweeters counter that Twitter isn't (or shouldn't be) a numbers game. Your friend timeline should be a reflection of your interests, your work life, or your social life (or even all three), and automatically adding tweeters to your list of friends defeats that purpose because you're bound to get deluged with updates you're completely uninterested in, or even offended by. Even worse, if you're lucky enough to become popular on Twitter, do you really want your timeline to be inundated with the tweets from hundreds or even thousands of users, the vast majority of whom you don't know from Adam?

Which side of the fence you come down on in this debate really depends on what you want to get out of Twitter. If you want to keep in touch with friends, family, and a few tweeters that you've found interesting or entertaining, then follow who you want; if you want the complete social experience that Twitter provides, follow everyone who comes your way.

Following someone who is following you

If you decide to go the latter route, then Twitter offers a couple of methods you can use to follow a person who is now following you:

- **E-mail link.** Assuming you've configured Twitter to send you an e-mail message each time someone follows you, display that message in your e-mail program, and then click the link to view the person's profile. When the profile loads in your Web browser, click the Follow button.

- **Twitter site.** Load your home page or profile page, click your followers link, and then click the Follow button beside the user.

Automatically following someone who follows you

Following your followers manually isn't a big deal if you only receive a few friend requests per day. However, if your Twitter profile takes off, you might become insanely popular and start receiving dozens of new followers each day. That's a nice position to be in, for sure, but you could end up spending vast chunks of your day just processing all those new fans.

To avoid that, you can use a powerful online tool called SocialOomph to automatically follow anyone who follows you. Go to www.socialoomph.com and sign up for a free registration. (There's a paid version of the service, but you don't need it for this.) Once you've done that, you add your Twitter account and then configure it to automatically follow your followers. Because SocialOomph is an online service, the interface changes fairly regularly. However, here are the steps to follow as I write this:

1. **Log on to your SocialOomph account.**
2. **Click the Accounts tab.**
3. **Click the Add Account tab.** The Add New Account page appears.
4. **Select the Twitter option and click Continue.** The Add a New Twitter Account page appears.
5. **Type your screen name in the Twitter User Name text box.**
6. **Type your password in the Twitter Password text box.**
7. **Type the Bot Prevention text.**
8. **Click Save.** SocialOomph saves your Twitter account info.

You can now activate the Auto Follow feature:

1. **Click the Accounts tab.**
2. **Click the Edit Automation tab.**
3. **Click the Edit link beside your Twitter account.** The Optional Twitter Account Automation page appears.
4. **Select the Auto Follow check box, as shown in figure G.**

5. **Click Save.** SocialOomph adds your accounts and configures it to automatically follow your followers.

Optional Twitter Account Automation	
Auto Welcome:	☑ Automatically send a welcome message to new followers.
Message Sending Method:	All welcome messages are sent as Direct Messages.
Send This Message:	[ ]
	Maximum 120 characters.
	Best Practise: The message should not be about you, it should be about your follower and your future interaction with your follower.
	Write a very simple welcome message. If you really want folks to unfollow you, then try and sell them something with this first welcome message. Very few people like that. Be careful even if you're giving away something for free. The purpose of this message is to say hello and welcome. Most people take a dim view of you when you do any kind of self-promotion with this message. If your message smells remotely like, "Hi, thanks for the follow, now buy my stuff or do something that will benefit me or check out how cool I am," then you really are misusing this welcome message. Don't send what you wouldn't like to receive from others.
Auto Follow:	☑ Automatically follow people (new followers) who follow me from this point forward.
Vet Followers:	☐

G Add your Twitter account to SocialOomph and select the Auto Follow check box.

Note

As I write this SocialOomph waits about 8 hours before processing your new followers, and it then checks your account a couple of times a day to look for new followers. SocialOomph does not process your existing followers, so if you want to follow them you must do it manually.

Downloading your friends' tweets

If you're a bit behind on your friends' updates and you're looking for a way to catch up while you're offline, this usually requires a Twitter client. However, if you're willing to wrestle with some XML code, then here's another method you can use:

1. **In your Web browser, type the following address, where you replace *n* with the number of updates you want to retrieve:**

http://twitter.com/statuses/friends_timeline.xml?count=*n*

2. **Press Enter or Return.** The Twitter server prompts you to log on to your account.

3. **Enter your Twitter username and password.** The browser displays the updates in XML format.

Stopping following someone on Twitter

Unfortunately, it's a fact of Twitter life that not everyone is interesting! Some people take the What are you doing? question too much to heart, some people are rude, and some people simply over share. Whatever the reason, if someone's updates are clogging your timeline, it's best to "defriend" that person by stopping following them. There are two ways you can do this:

- **Viewing your list of followers.** Sign in to your account, click either Home or Profile, and then click Followers. Locate the person you want to get rid of, click the Actions button (the gear icon) beside that person's info, and then click the Unfollow username command, where username is the Twitter name of the person you want to remove (figure H shows an example).

- **Viewing a person's profile page.** In this case, click the Actions button and then click the Unfollow username command, where username is the person's Twitter name.

Click the user's Actions button and then click the Unfollow command.

Replying, Retweeting, and Direct Messaging

Twitter is a social network, and part of what that entails is the exchange of messages between tweeters. This is mostly achieved by posting updates that then appear on the friend timelines of the folks who follow you, but Twitter also offers three other ways to create conversations and exchanges: replying to an update; retweeting an update; and sending someone a direct message. The next three sections tackle the specifics.

Replying to an update

A *reply* is a response to a tweeter's update, and that response appears on your timeline, as well as on the original tweeter's timeline. You usually send replies to people you follow, but on Twitter anyone can send a reply to anyone (as long as that person's account isn't protected). Send a reply when you have a comment about a tweet, you want to follow up on a tweet, or you have new information about a tweet.

Here are the steps to follow to reply to an update:

1. **Sign in to your Twitter account.**
2. **Locate the update you want to reply to.** The update might appear on your friend timeline, in your mentions timeline, a tweeter's timeline, the Twitter public timeline, or in the result of a Twitter search.
3. **If the update appears in a timeline, hover the mouse pointer over the update.** Twitter displays the Reply link and the Reply to *username* banner (where *username* is the name of the person who posted the tweet; see figure J). If the update appears in a list of Twitter search results, you see a Reply arrow instead.

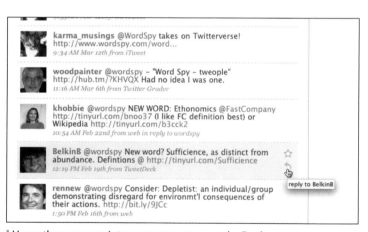

karma_musings @WordSpy takes on Twitterverse!
http://www.wordspy.com/word...
9:34 AM Mar 12th from iTweet

woodpainter @wordspy – "Word Spy – tweople"
http://hub.tm/?KHVQX Had no idea I was one.
11:16 AM Mar 6th from Twitter Grader

khobbie @wordspy NEW WORD: Ethonomics @FastCompany
http://tinyurl.com/bnoo37 (I like FC definition best) or
Wikipedia http://tinyurl.com/b3cck2
10:54 AM Feb 22nd from web in reply to wordspy

BelkinB @wordspy New word? Sufficience, as distinct from
abundance. Defintions @ http://tinyurl.com/Sufficience
12:19 PM Feb 19th from TweetDeck

reply to BelkinB

rennew @wordspy Consider: Depletist: an individual/group
demonstrating disregard for environmt'l consequences of
their actions. http://bit.ly/9JCc
1:50 PM Feb 16th from web

I Hover the mouse pointer over a tweet to see the Reply arrow.

4. **Click the Reply arrow.** If you're working with search results, click the Reply arrow instead. Twitter displays the Reply to *username* text box and adds @*username* to the box (where, in both cases, *username* is the tweeter's screen name).
5. **Type your reply as shown in figure J.** Feel free to add text either before or after the @*username* text. Twitter will recognize the tweet as a reply as long as you have the @*username* text somewhere within the update

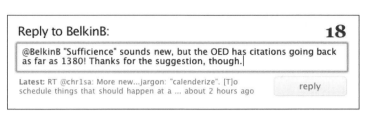

J Type your response in the Reply to *username* text box.

6. **Click Reply.** Twitter posts the reply, which then appears in your update timeline as well as in the user's mentions timeline.

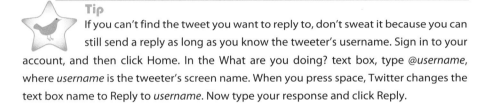

Tip

If you can't find the tweet you want to reply to, don't sweat it because you can still send a reply as long as you know the tweeter's username. Sign in to your account, and then click Home. In the What are you doing? text box, type *@username*, where *username* is the tweeter's screen name. When you press space, Twitter changes the text box name to Reply to *username*. Now type your response and click Reply.

Sending a reply to all your followers

When you send a reply (or any tweet that begins with *@username*), the resulting tweet appears in your profile timeline and in the friend timeline of the person you replied to. What about the people you follow? You normally see their tweets in your friend timeline, but do you also see the replies they send out to other people? The answer is that it depends on who they reply to:

● If a person you follow replies to another person you follow, then the reply shows up in your friend timeline.

● If a person you follow replies to a person you don't follow, then the reply does *not* appear in your friend timeline.

This configuration makes sense when you think about it. For example, suppose you follow Kyra and David, and Kyra replies to one of David's tweets. Because you're following both people, chances are you saw David's tweet that Kyra replied to, so you probably understand (or can figure out) what her reply means. Therefore, it's reasonable for you to see Kyra's reply on your friend timeline.

On the other hand, suppose you follow Kyra but not David. In this case, you didn't see David's original tweet, so Kyra's reply might be gibberish. It, therefore, makes sense for the reply to not appear on your friend timeline.

However, there may be times you want to reply to someone and you want that reply to be seen by *all* the people who follow you. After all, if your reply contains useful, relevant, or fun info, why shouldn't you share it with all your friends? Twitter offers no feature to handle this kind of scenario directly, but as is often the case with Twitter, the users have come up with their own solution.

The trick is to include @*username* anywhere in the tweet *except* the beginning. Twitter then treats it like a regular update and ships it to all your followers. So, to send a reply that's seen by all your followers, start the response with a single character such as a dot (.), a tilde (~), or something similarly non-intrusive. Then type the @*username*, followed by your response text. The resulting tweet *looks* like a reply, but all your followers see your wise or witty riposte.

Retweeting an update

A *retweet* is another person's tweet that you send to your followers. You most often retweet updates from the people you follow, but you can retweet anyone's updates. Retweet an update if you think it will be especially interesting or relevant to the people who follow you.

Here are the steps to follow to retweet to an update:

1. **Sign in to your Twitter account.**
2. **Locate the update you want to retweet.** The update might appear on your friend timeline, in your mentions timeline, a tweeter's timeline, or the Twitter public timeline.
3. **Hover the mouse pointer over the update.** Twitter displays the Retweet link.
4. **Click the Retweet link.** Twitter displays a dialog box asking you to confirm that you want to retweet the update to all your followers.
5. **Click Yes.** Twitter posts the retweet, which then appears in your profile timeline as well as in the timelines of all your followers.

Tip

Oddly, as I write this Twitter doesn't let you directly retweet an update that appears in results of a Twitter search. To retweet a search result, you have to first display the tweet itself. You do that by clicking the "ago" link that tells you how long ago the update was posted (such as 2 minutes ago or 1 day ago).

A few extra tidbits tell you that this is a retweet instead of a regular update:

- The original tweeter's avatar and username appear along with the tweet.

- The original tweeter's username is preceded by the retweet icon.

- The relative time shown with the tweet is the time of the original update, not the retweet.

- You see the message retweeted by *username* and *x* others, where *username* is the person who retweeted the update, and *x* is the number of other people who have retweeted the same update.

What I've just described in the "official" Twitter method of retweeting an update. There is, however, an "unofficial" method that's still quite common, so you need to know about it. The *organic* retweet (as Twitter HQ insists on calling it) is a feature that was developed by the Twitter community a while back, and it became a standard part of the tweeter's posting arsenal. An organic retweet is an update that uses the following general form:

```
RT @username: original tweet [your comment]
```

Here, *username* is the name of the original tweeter; *original tweet* is the text of the update you're retweeting; and *your comment* is text that you add to comment on the update. Remember that this format isn't the only way to retweet. Some folks add their comments to the beginning; some people put the username at the end, while others use "retweet" or "retweeting" instead of RT.

Here's the basic procedure for retweeting an update using the RT method:

1. **Sign in to your Twitter account.**
2. **Locate the update you want to retweet.** The update might appear on your friend timeline, in your mentions timeline, a tweeter's timeline, the Twitter public timeline, or in the result of a Twitter search.
3. **Copy the tweet text, including the username at the beginning of the tweet.**
4. **Click Home.**
5. **Click inside the What's happening? text box.**
6. **Type RT.**
7. **Type a space and then @.**
8. **Paste the text you copied in step 3.**

9. **Type your own text (if you have room) after the original tweet text.**

10. **Click Update.** Twitter posts the retweet, which then appears in your update timeline.

Note

To keep track of the most popular retweets and the most retweeted users, check out Retweetist at http://retweetist.com.

Note

What if you come across a tweet that contains an interesting idea or a useful link, but you don't want to quote the original tweeter verbatim? For example, you might have your own spin on the original topic and so you want to post your thoughts along with the link. In that case, it's proper Twitter etiquette to acknowledge the original tweeter by including somewhere in your update the text "via *@username*", where *username* is the screen name of the original tweeter.

Okay, so you want to know what retweet feature to use, the official Twitter retweet feature or the organic RT method? The answer is that it depends:

- Use the official retweet method if you don't want to add a comment to the retweet, or if the original retweet is so long that it won't fit into an RT update without serious editing.

- Use the old-fashioned RT method if you want to include your .02 worth when you retweet.

Viewing your retweets

By definition, retweets are updates that you found fascinating enough or funny enough to pass along to your posse. So it stands to reason that you might want to check out a particular retweet later on to relive the moment. If you used the official Twitter retweet method, then you're in luck because Twitter keeps track of your retweets. Here's how to get at them:

1. **Sign in to your Twitter account.**

2. **Click Home.**

3. **In the sidebar, click Retweets.** Twitter takes you to the retweets page.

4. **Click the Retweets By You tab.** Twitter displays a list of your retweets, as shown in figure K.

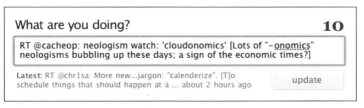

K Click the Retweets By You tab to see your retweets.

Sending a direct message to someone

A *direct message* is a note that you send directly to a tweeter, where "direct" means that the message doesn't appear on either your timeline or the recipient's timeline. You can only send a direct message to someone if the two of you follow each other. Send a direct message when you want a private exchange with someone.

How you send a direct message depends on where you are in the Twitter landscape:

- If you're viewing the list of people you follow, you see a Direct message link beside each person that also follows you. Click the Direct message link for the person you want to contact.

- If you're on the profile page of a mutual follower, click the Message link in the Actions section of the sidebar.

- If you're viewing your Direct Messages timeline (click Home and then click Direct Messages in the sidebar), use the Send *x* a direct message list to choose your recipient (see figure L).

Whichever message you use, Twitter displays a text box. Type your message in the box, as shown in figure L, and then click Send.

L After you choose your recipient, type the message and click Send.

If you're having a hard time finding the person you want to direct message, you don't need to use the Twitter interface to find them. If you know the person's username, you can click

Home and use the What are you doing? text box to type a message that uses the following general format:

```
d username message
```

Here, *username* is the screen name of the person you want to write to, and *message* is your text. When your message is ready, click Send to ship it.

Finally, if someone sends you a direct message, you might feel like writing back. The easiest way to do this is through your Direct Messages timeline (click Home, and then click Direct Messages in the sidebar). Hover the mouse over the message you want to respond to; then click the envelope icon shown in figure M. Type your response in the text box and then click Send.

M Hover the mouse pointer over a direct message to see the envelope (reply) icon.

note

To keep your Direct Messages timeline less cluttered, delete any messages you no longer need. Hover the mouse pointer over the message, and then click the trash can icon. When Twitter asks you to confirm the deletion, click OK.

Configuring direct message e-mails

When you follow someone and that person also follows you, then the two of you can send direct messages to each other. Because direct messages are more personal, Twitter automatically configures your account to send any direct messages you receive to your e-mail address. If you want to turn off this feature, or if you like the idea and want to make sure this setting is activated, follow these steps:

1. **Sign in to your Twitter account.**

2. **Click Settings.** Your Twitter account settings appear.

3. **Click the Notices tab.**

4. **To get direct messages via e-mail, select the Direct Text Emails check box.**

5. **Click Save.** Twitter configures your account with the new setting.

Working with the People You Follow

Once you start following people on Twitter, your interactions with them will mostly consist of reading their tweets, replying when you've got something to say, and sending direct messages to people who also follow you. However, Twitter does offer a few other choices, such as displaying a person's updates and nudging and blocking a user. The next few sections provide the details.

Checking out a person's updates

If you follow a bunch of people, a particular update from a particular user can fall off the first page of your friend timeline in a hurry. Rather than leaping through your timeline pages to locate the tweet, it's often easier to display the person's updates. This is also useful if you've been offline (or just off-Twitter) for a while and you want to catch up with a favorite friend.

Twitter gives you several ways to access a user's tweet timeline, depending on where you are in the interface:

- If you see an update from that person in your friend timeline, click the username at the start of the tweet.
- If you've got the person onscreen in your list of followers, click the username.
- Use your Web browser to type **http://twitter.com/*username***, where *username* is the Twitter screen name of the person you want to read.

Preventing a person's retweets from appearing in your timeline

Earlier you learned how to send a retweet the official Twitter way by clicking the Retweet link beside an update. This is a great way to share tweet gold with your followers. Hopefully some of your friends are also retweeting, because it's one of the best ways to find interesting Twitterers. However, in the world of retweets there's sharing and then there's *over*-sharing. Some folks seem to think that nine out of every ten tweets they receive are retweet-worthy, so your regular friend timeline gets inundated with a bunch of recycled (and usually uninteresting) updates.

If a particular Twitterer's retweet habit is sticking in your craw, help is just around the corner. Twitter offers a setting that enables you to block all the retweets sent by someone you follow. (Note that this setting only works with official retweets; the old-fashioned RT-style retweets aren't affected.) Here are the steps to follow to block someone's retweets:

1. **Sign in to your Twitter account.**

2. **Navigate the home page of the person whose retweets you want to block.** You can do this either by clicking the Following link in your sidebar and then clicking the user's name, or by navigating directly to twitter.com/username. When you get to the user's page, look for the Retweet icon to the right of the Following indicator.

5. **Click the Retweet icon.** The icon turns from green to white to indicate that you will no longer receive that person's retweets. To make sure, hover the mouse pointer over the icon.

Viewing your friends' retweets

As I mentioned before, when someone you follow retweets an update, that retweet shows up in your friend timeline. And, of course, just like a regular update, that retweet slowly (or sometimes quickly) gets buried under the incessant accumulation of new tweets. Since retweets are quite often interesting or useful, wouldn't it be nice if there was some easy to locate a retweet later on?

As I also mentioned before, a retweet doesn't appear in your friend timeline if you've already seen the update (because the original was posted by someone you follow). That prevents you from having to wade through duplicate tweets, but sometimes it's useful to know that one of your friends' updates is being retweeted hither and thither. Wouldn't it be nice if there was some easy way to see these hidden retweets?

I also told you earlier that when you see a retweet in your timeline, the update says "Retweeted by *username* and *x* others," where *username* is the name of the retweeter, and *x* is the number of times the original update has been through the retweet mill. Wouldn't it be nice if there was some easy way to find out who else has retweeted the update?

Fortunately, the answer to each of the three not-so-musical questions posed in the previous three paragraphs is "Yes!" Twitter maintains a complete list of all the updates that people you follow have retweeted. This list includes not only the retweets that you saw in your timeline, but also the hidden retweets where you saw the originals. The list also shows you the avatars of each person who has retweeted the update. Here's how to see this list:

1. **Sign in to your Twitter account.**

2. **Click Home.**

3. **In the sidebar, click Retweets.** Twitter takes you to the retweets page.

4. **Click the Retweets By Others tab.** Twitter displays a list of your friends retweets.

Viewing your tweets that have been retweeted

There aren't many chances in life to get our egos stroked, even for a short time, but Twitter can help because you get a nice little ego boost every time some kind soul retweets one of your updates. For an even bigger shot of self esteem, check out the complete list of your updates that have been retweeted:

1. **Sign in to your Twitter account.**

2. **Click Home.**

3. **In the sidebar, click Retweets.** Twitter takes you to the retweets page.

4. **Click the Your Tweets, Retweeted tab.** Twitter displays a list of all your updates that have been retweeted.

Blocking a tweeter

A huge number of people use Twitter, and most of those folks seem to get the friendly Twitter vibe. Of course, anytime you're dealing with a massive crowd you're bound to come across a bad apple or three. It might be someone who's rude or offensive, a huckster using Twitter to sell snake oil, or a company that bombards you with marketing messages. In most cases, the easiest solution is to stop following the user and, if the user is also following you, to remove the person from your list of followers.

That usually works, but there's a small subset of pests who'll just start following you all over again, or who'll send you replies even if they're not following you. For these hardcore cases, Twitter offers a hardcore solution: block the user. Blocking someone means that he or she can't follow you and can't send you replies.

Twitter gives you two ways to block a user:

- If the person is currently following you, open your list of followers, click the person's Actions button, and then click Block *username*.

- If the person isn't following you, go to his or her profile page and click Block *username* in the Actions section of the sidebar, as shown in figure N.

Actions

block tonyrobbins

⋔ To shut annoying tweeters out of your life, access their profile page, click Actions, and then click Block *username*.

Working with Twitter Bots

Twitter is home to millions of people, but it's also a place where many non-humans hang out. Yes, there are lots of companies and organizations on Twitter, but I'm talking here about a different kind of Twitter critter: the bot. A *bot* is an automated Twitter account that returns some kind of data in response to a specially formatted message. Some Twitter bots respond to reply messages, but most require direct messages, which means that you must follow the bot, and the bot then automatically follows you. (Remember that direct messaging requires mutual following. If you've protected your account, be sure to accept the bot's friend request when it comes in.)

In the rest of this chapter, I introduce you to Twitter's bot population by showing you how to interact with a few of the more useful bots.

Note
Twitter bots are most useful when you've configured your account to send direct messages to you, either via e-mail (as described earlier in this chapter) or via your mobile phone.

Receiving a reminder message

Ask someone how they're doing these days, and more often than not you'll get an exasperated "Busy!" as the response. We're all up to our eyeballs in meetings, chores, and other commitments, so it's not surprising that every now and then we forget one of those tasks, and all the apologizing we have to do puts us even farther behind. Fortunately, you can use Twitter to avoid this fate. The Twitter bot named timer is an automated reminder service. You send it a direct message and a time, and when that time elapses timer sends you a direct message back.

To use timer, first go to http://twitter.com/timer and click the Follow button to follow this bot; it immediately follows you in return, so you're now set up to exchange direct messages with timer.

When you need a reminder, send a direct message to timer with the number of minutes after which you want the reminder sent (the minimum is 5 minutes), and the text you want timer to send back in the reminder message. For example, if you want to be reminded to call Karen in 30 minutes, your direct message will look like this:

```
30 Call Karen
```

If you're using the What are you doing? text box to send the message, remember to include the d command and the timer username:

```
d timer 30 Call Karen
```

Caution

The timer bot is useful, but don't rely on it for accurate reminders. The timer bot seems to get around to sending the reminders when it's good and ready, so reminders are routinely a few minutes late.

Querying the Internet Movie Database

If you want to get some quick info on a movie or a movie personality, the famous Internet Movie Database (www.imdb.com) has a Twitter bot — named, not surprisingly, imdb — that's happy to serve. The imdb bot responds to either direct messages or reply messages.

To use direct messages, go to http://twitter.com/imdb and click the Follow button; the imdb bot follows you right back. Note, too, that the imdb account on Twitter also tweets regularly by sending out movie-related updates with themes such as Born On This Date, Trivia, and Quote.

If you don't want to receive the imdb tweets, bypass the following and send messages to @imdb instead.

If you want to get information about a movie, use the t command followed by the name of the movie:

```
d imdb t spinal tap
```

or

```
@imdg t spinal tap
```

If you know there are multiple versions of the movie, you can also specify the year:

```
d imdb t gladiator 2000
```

or

```
@imdb t gladiator 2000
```

To get information about a movie personality, use the p command followed by the person's name:

```
d imdb p clive owen
```

or

```
@imdb p clive owen
```

Getting a map

If you need a quick map of a city or town, use the Twitter 411 bot named t411. Go to http://twitter.com/t411 and click the Follow button; the t411 bot immediately follows you, too. You can now send your request using the following format:

```
d t411 map place
```

Here, *place* is the name of the city or town you want to see on a map. In response, you get a direct message with a URL. Click that address to see the map.

Translating text into another language

If you want to know how to say an English word or phrase in French, German, or some other language, or if you come across a foreign phrase that you want to convert to English, you can use the Twitter bot named twanslate. This is a direct message bot, so you first need to go to http://twitter.com/twanslate and click the Follow button. Once twanslate follows you back, you're good to go.

The first thing you should do is retrieve the twanslate help text by sending the following direct message:

```
d twanslate help
```

This text gives you the language abbreviations that you need to use in the twanslate commands. For example, the abbreviation for French is fr, so to translate the English phrase "I love Twitter" into French, you'd send the following message:

```
d twanslate fr I love Twitter
```

Getting a weather forecast

Want to know what the weather's going to be like where you are or where you're traveling to, but don't have access to a weather forecast? Now you do thanks to the Twitter bot named forecast, which can provide a forecast for a given city or a given postal code.

The forecast bot uses direct messages, so first navigate to http://twitter.com/forecast and click the Follow button. Once the forecast bot returns the following favor, you can send your message. There are two ways to use the forecast bot: by city and by postal code.

To get the weather forecast for a city, send a direct message with the following format:

```
d forecast city, state
```

Replace *city* with the name of the city, and replace *state* with the two-letter state abbreviation. For example, the following direct message returns the forecast for Indianapolis, Indiana:

```
d forecast indianapolis, in
```

To get a weather forecast for a particular ZIP or postal code, send a direct message with the following format:

```
d forecast zip
```

Here, replace *zip* with the ZIP code of the location. For example, the following direct message returns the forecast for the 46256:

```
d forecast 46256
```

Returning Amazon data

Amazon.com stores a wealth of data about millions of books, DVDs, and albums, and now all of that data is at your fingertips thanks to the Twitter bot named junglebot. This bot responds to direct messages, so first go to http://twitter.com/junglebot and click the Follow button. Once junglebot follows you back, you can use it to start querying Amazon.

You can use junglebot to return data about books, DVDs, or music using the following direct messages formats:

```
d junglebot book title
d junglebot dvd title
d junglebot music title
```

In each case, replace *title* with the name of the book, DVD, or music CD you want to work with. For example, to get information about the book *iPhone 3G Portable Genius*, you'd send the following direct message:

```
d junglebot book iphone 3g portable genius
```

Keeping up with the bots

The half dozen bots that you learn about here really only scratch the surface of a burgeoning new Twitter field. New bots seem to come online every day, so how do you keep up? Perhaps the best way is the Twittter Fan Wiki, a wiki site that monitors all-things Twitter, including bots. Check out the following page from time to time to see what's new in the Twitter bot landscape:

http://twitter.pbworks.com/Bots

glossary

avatar The user icon associated with a Twitter account.

badge A small graphic with a Twitter-inspired design that you use as a link to your Twitter home page.

bot An automated Twitter account that returns some kind of data in response to a specially formatted message.

celebritweet A celebrity or famous person who uses Twitter.

direct To send a direct message to someone; a direct message.

direct message A private note that only the recipient can read.

exactotweet See *twoosh*.

fail whale The page that Twitter displays when it is over capacity and can't accept any more tweets.

followership The people who follow a particular Twitter user.

followorthy Worthy of being followed on Twitter.

hashtag A word that, when preceded by a hash (#), defines or references a topic on Twitter.

hypertweeting Posting an excessive number of tweets.

live-tweeting Sending on-the-fly updates that describe or summarize some ongoing event.

mashup Information created by combining data from two or more different sources.

meme A cultural artifact, such as an idea or catchphrase, that spreads quickly from person to person.

microblogging Posting short thoughts and ideas to an online site such as Twitter.

mutual follow When two people on Twitter follow each other.

nudge A text message sent to your phone to remind you to post an update.

partial retweet A retweet that includes only part of the original tweet.

reply A response to a tweeter's update.

retweet Another person's tweet that you copy and send out to your followers, along with an acknowledgment of the original tweeter.

RT An abbreviation used to mark an update as a retweet; a retweet.

timeline A related collection of tweets, sorted by the date and time they were posted.

tweeple People who use Twitter.

tweeps A Twitter user's friends.

tweet An update posted to Twitter.

tweet cred Twitter credibility.

tweeter A person who uses Twitter.

tweetstream The tweets in a timeline.

tweetup A real-world meeting between two or more people who know each other through the online Twitter service.

tweetwalking Writing and posting a Twitter update while walking.

tweme A Twitter meme.

tweople See *tweeple*.

Twitosphere See *Twitterverse*.

Twittaholic A person who uses Twitter compulsively.

Twitterer A Twitter user.

Twitterati The Twitter users with the most followers and influence.

Twitterpated Overwhelmed by incoming tweets.

Twitterrhea The act of posting an excessive number of tweets in a short time.

Twittersphere See *Twitterverse*.

Twitterverse The Twitter social networking service and the people who use it.

Twitterstream See *tweetstream*.

Twitticism A witty tweet.

Twittiquette Twitter etiquette; an informal set of guidelines and suggestions for updating, following, replying, and sending direct messages.

twoosh A tweet that is exactly 140 characters long.

tword A new word created by appending "tw" to an existing word.

URL shortening service A Web site or program that converts a Web address into a much shorter URL and then uses that URL to redirect users to the original address.

index

Index

Index

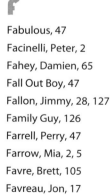

Index

Index

Index

Index

Index

Index